···· THE ····
SWEETAPOLITA
B·A·K·E·B·O·O·K

Clarkson Potter/Publishers

New York

····THE····
SWEETAPOLITA
B·A·K·E·B·O·O·K

75 Fanciful Cakes, Cookies &
More to Make & Decorate

ROSIE ALYEA

Published in the United States by Clarkson Potter/Publishers, an imprint of
the Crown Publishing Group, a division of Random House LLC, a Penguin
Random House Company, New York.
www.crownpublishing.com
www.clarksonpotter.com

CLARKSON POTTER is a trademark and POTTER with colophon is a
registered trademark of Random House LLC.

All photographs excluding those on pages 8, 9, and 11 are by the author.
Photograph on page 9 courtesy of the author

Library of Congress Cataloging-in-Publication Data
Alyea, Rosie.
  The Sweetapolita Bakebook / Rosie Alyea. — First edition.
    pages   cm
  Includes index.
1. Cake.   2. Cookies.   3. Cake decorating.   I. Title.
TX771.A494 2015
641.81'5—dc23   2014018092

ISBN 978-0-7704-3531-8
eBook ISBN 978-0-7704-3532-5

Printed in China

Book and cover design by Rae Ann Spitzenberger
Cover photography by Rosie Alyea

10 9 8 7 6 5 4 3 2 1

First Edition

To my cakelets, Reese Amelia and Neve Winter—
by far the most splendid delights I will ever create.

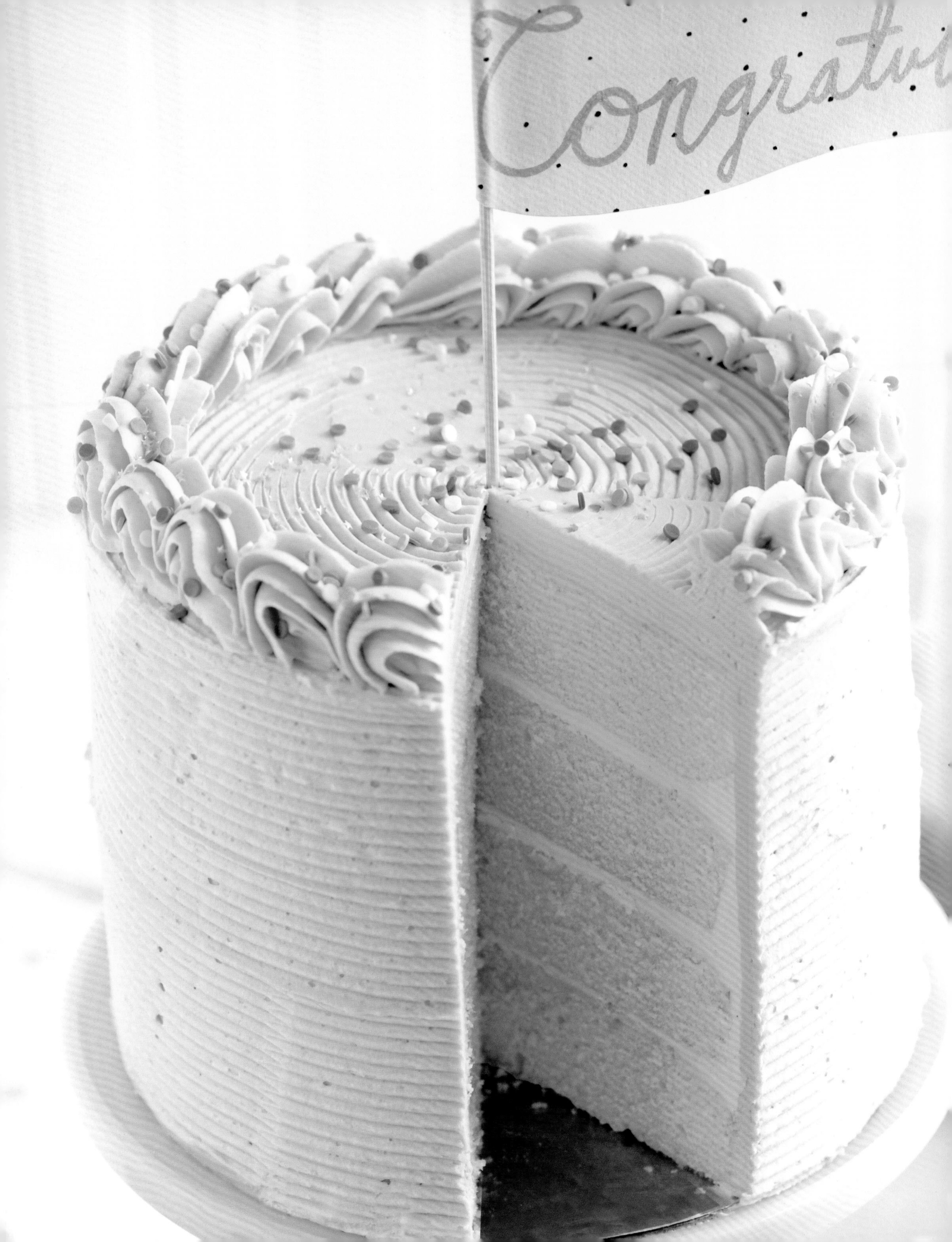

CONTENTS

INTRODUCTION

I CAN STILL VIVIDLY RECALL MY FIRST CAKE EXPERIENCE: It was 1977, and I was earnestly leaning over a heart-shaped chocolate birthday cake, feeling the warmth of three little pink Cake Mate candles burning away as I excitedly tried to dream up a wish. The cake was adorned with stark-white and Barbie-pink frosting roses, swirly piped borders, and an elegantly scripted "Happy Birthday Rosanne." It was the quintessential supermarket bakery cake, and it was perfect. My mom was never much of a cake-baker, though she always cooked big meals and made many a pie.

For many years to follow, my mom bought me these beloved heart-shaped birthday cakes—sometimes chocolate, more often vanilla—from our local grocery store in my hometown of Kitchener, Ontario. She knew, as mothers do, that something as simple as a cake had the power to make her little girl's eyes twinkle and smile shine brighter. To this day, I cannot spot a heart-shaped cake, or even a heart-shaped cake pan, without feeling the love and comfort of my childhood.

When I was sixteen, as a result of pure serendipity, I got a job at the only fancy bakery in our city, and it was during that time that I (officially) fell in love with the world-and-wonder of cake and confection. Despite having a longtime enchantment with pretty baked goods, my "cake" career began in a much different way when, in my twenties, I partnered with a friend and created a successful dessert-themed bath and body product company called Cake Beauty. And although I left the thriving company in 2003, I believe that those were the formative years of what later became Sweetapolita. A few

years later, after getting married and having our first little cakelet, Reese, I was shopping and randomly came across *The Confetti Cakes Cookbook* by Elisa Strauss. As I flipped through the pages, I felt these pangs of envy and sparks of motivation, and—BAM—just like that I knew it was time to follow my heart and finally learn how to professionally bake and decorate fancy cakes. The next day, I registered for baking and cake design courses at Bonnie Gordon College of Confectionary Arts in Toronto. It was there that I was lucky enough to learn from some of the world's leading cake artists and ultimately became a professional baker and cake designer. After weeks of feverish brainstorming, I came up with the name Sweetapolita—a nonsense word that would represent my playful approach to baking and hopefully capture the essence of my work—and with this name, I started my own custom cake and confection business.

Initially, I assumed that I would continue to pursue life as a wedding cake designer, but as much as I loved creating pretty desserts, something was missing. It was right around that time that I took a quick wedding cake photography workshop, with the simple hopes of learning to snap some decent shots of my creations to build a cake design portfolio. But then something unexpected happened: I fell hard and fast for food photography, or, well, "cake photography" (let's make that a thing). All I wanted to do was bake cakes and photograph them, and I was so inspired that I would talk about baking all day and night to anyone who would listen.

So with this burning desire, I decided to up and start a blog. I realized that if I had my own website, I would have a reason to make-a-cake, photograph, and write all about it—anytime I wanted. I had no idea who would actually read it, but it really didn't matter at that point. It just seemed like the perfect way to immerse myself in the world of bakers and other artistic folk. My creative heart and soul were all a-sparkle as I launched Sweetapolita.com.

But of course it's not just about career happiness. To me, baking is so, so much more than that. Frolicking in flour and frosting, even as a hobby or occasional pastime, is something that no one can ever take away from you. It is yours. Baking is timeless, its possibilities are boundless, and you can infuse it with your own flair—most often delighting everyone in your path along the way. Like a magic wand filled with sugar and sprinkles, sharing a made-with-love dessert seems to have the almighty power to instantly provide a sense of glee. A single confection can transport someone straight back to his or her childhood—often before even a spoonful of frosting or single cake crumb is tasted. Add a few unexpected touches of whimsy-and-wow to your creations, and you just might teleport them somewhere they've never even been.

As much as we love to bake for others, the truth is, I think there is just as much in it for us—or more. There's something empowering about spending time alone with your creativity and making something with your own two hands, and I strongly believe that we all yearn to leave our stamp on the world— whatever it may be. Whether it's blogging, opening a bakeshop, having a career in custom cake designing, or even simply being the noted baker of the family, I believe you can thrive if you set out to be different and memorable. I mean, since we're in this, let's do what we love, kick it up a notch, and make some serious magic!

Throughout this book, you will find that most of the recipes and ideas are geared to tickle the childhood fancy in all of us while serving up a slight dose of drama and sense of splendor, making them suitable for anything from coffee with friends to the fanciest of celebrations or events. While working on this book, I strived to create desserts that you just might find if you discovered an enchanting bakery tucked away within some distant candy-colored carnival, because I can't help but feel that a dash-of-dreamy makes

Cookies, page 69) to cotton candy (Pink Cotton Candy Cloud Cookies, page 75).

But creating the For the Love of Layer Cakes chapter allowed me to embrace my obsession for layer cakes. The enchanting lavender and blueberry Blue Moon Dream Cake (page 85) celebrates supreme flavors and textures, while the four-layer Double-Chocolate Birthday Cake (page 82) revels in serious chocolate decadence, but with a decorative twist. And since some parties require even more cake (my kind of party!), I created an entire chapter of tiered cakes—Fanciful Tiered Cakes, to be exact—in which I share some of my favorite fondant and buttercream techniques, such as creating a beaded effect (Beads & Baubles Cake, page 117), twinkly sequins (Sprinkle Twinkle Cake, page 112), and a chalkboard finish (Chalk-a-Lot Cake, page 111) that is ready to be doodled upon with bright Edible Chalk (page 54).

I also created the ultimate building blocks for successful baking and caking: the last few chapters include my prized basics, including lofty, tender cakes for layering, the fluffiest of frostings, the most decadent fillings, and ever-buttery-and-crisp rolled cookie recipes, as well as many favorite fundamental cake-decorating techniques, such as frosting the perfect layer cake, covering a cake in fondant, and more. These recipes and techniques are not only used to create many of the designs in the book, but can be mixed and matched to create countless new dessert ideas—fancy cakes and confections aplenty!

And whether you bake for whim or for work, I sincerely hope that this book inspires you to bake yourself happy, let your imagination run the show, and delight all of those lucky people around you.

Love,
Rosie xo

everything taste better. As a sprinkle-junkie, I couldn't resist devoting an entire chapter to sprinkles. With recipes such as Sprinkle-Me-Silly Pizza (page 22) and Rainbows & Sprinkles Cake (page 34), I celebrate the diversity and merriment of the sprinkle—hooray! While many recipes in this book call to the child in all of us, children are the focus of the playful Wondrous Desserts for the Wee chapter, where we help kids dive into super-colorful and creativity-inducing recipes like the Cut & Paste Illustration Cake (page 55) and Chalk-a-Lot Cookies with Edible Chalk (page 53). And who says cookies are just for kids? Things get a bit fancier in the Sugar-Coated Cutout Cookies chapter—classic cutout cookies are adorned with everything from glittery sugar (Menagerie Masquerade

SPRINKLES
SPECTACULAR!

GUIDE TO SPRINKLES

Sprinkles! Where there are sprinkles, there is happiness. I doubt I have to convince you that sprinkles make life better, but what *is* a sprinkle? A sprinkle is any small (or not so small) bit of sugar in one of countless forms that's used to add decorative flair, texture, and sometimes taste to baked goods, frozen treats, and more. I'd say I'm a sprinkle purist in that I believe they should not only add serious eye appeal but must also be made of sugar—or at least contain some form of sugar (or, heck, even *pretend* to contain sugar).

I don't think that just the *act* of sprinkling something onto a baked good makes it a sprinkle. Now, there are some exceptions—anything twinkly, such as edible gold or silver stars and flakes, might not taste like much, but I still consider them sprinkles of sorts, because their entire purpose in life is to add fanciness to our baked goods. But whoa . . . not so fast, Mister Fancy Salt: you're tasty, but you simply aren't a sprinkle. To navigate this arena, I've come up with two groups of sprinkles: the sweet and tasty variety (tasty bits, balls, and beads) and the lovely-but-flavorless variety (decorative doodads). For information on where to find these pretty decorations, see Sources on page 203.

TASTY BITS, BALLS, AND BEADS

Candy Beads: These fancy sprinkles taste just as their name suggests. They are a perfect pea size and are tasty and delicious. They come in a wide variety of vibrant colors, as well as in a larger size, which are actually candy-coated chocolate candies, much like Sixlets.

Candy Shapes: These sweet shapes come in every shape, from neon stars to colorful tiny fruits. These little bits are basically candy that has graduated to sprinkle status.

Crushed Candy or Cookies: While these aren't exactly sprinkles, they do count! Pretty much any crushed-up cookie or candy can instantly become a sprinkle: try candy canes, chocolate wafers, and lollipops.

Glitter Sugar: I kind of made this one up. Sometimes you want the yummy crunch of sanding sugar, but with way more dazzle. So I shake up a container of disco dust for every 2 cups or so of sanding sugar—suddenly we have glittery sugar.

Jimmies: These long, slender, often rainbow-colored bits are one of the most commonly used sprinkles. After many reader emails about where I find the "pretty jimmies that are so long and skinny," I realized that jimmies manufactured in Canada are indeed quite long and skinny, and those manufactured in the United States are noticeably chubbier and shorter. Who knew? Try my Homemade Sprinkles recipe on page 16, which produces a Canadian-style sprinkle.

Nonpareils: Ah, the sprinkles of my childhood. These ultra-tiny round balls are available in rainbow variety or in single colors, and they are crunchy, sweet, and sugary. The colorful bits are known in the United Kingdom, Australia, and New Zealand as "hundreds and thousands" (accidentally drop a jar of these on the floor, and you'll know what they're referring to).

Quins (aka Confetti Quins or Edible Confetti): When baking confetti cupcakes or cake, you'll find these slender discs work best, as they don't bleed color or sink to the bottom. They are available in a wide variety of shapes, even including animals, as well as in a jumbo size.

DECORATIVE DOODADS

Disco Dust: This powdery, super-sparkly glitter is certainly the most dazzling of the sprinkle family. This is as twinkly as it gets, truly. It comes in almost any color or shade you can dream up and adds serious glamour. While disco dust is deemed nontoxic, it's best to not ingest excessive quantities but, rather, to use it for dazzling details.

Dragées: These metallic balls of varying sizes typically come from Italy. They are usually crunchy with a sweet taste, and they range in size from 2 to 6 millimeters (1/16 to 1/4 inch).

Edible Glitter: This term can mean one of two things, depending on the manufacturer. The glitter made by CK Products is light flakes of shimmery, glasslike pieces. This is quite different from disco dust (see above), but in some cases retailers will sell disco dust labeled as edible glitter.

Gold Flakes: Much like the Metallic Stars, these flakey bits add glamour to your treats with no taste or sweetness. Typically, though, these are 24 karat gold flakes and, naturally, cost quite a bit.

Metallic Stars: These tiny star-shaped flakes come in silver and gold, and while they don't taste like much, they definitely jazz up a dessert in a hurry.

Sugar Pearls: Pearly beauties, these come in an array of colors and many sizes, but many of them don't have much taste.

Sanding Sugar (aka Sparkling Sugar): Ooh, how I love this stuff. Essentially, this is just coarse white sugar, and it adds an addictive sugary crunch and subtle sparkle to cakes, cupcakes, and cookies. It is readily available in a wide variety of colors in baking supply and cake-decorating shops, but it is extremely simple to color your own (see page 16).

Sixlets: These substantial colorful balls are a mega-sprinkle of sorts. Candy-covered chocolate candy with a hard candy shell, they are perfect for topping cakes and cupcakes because they are as tasty as they are pretty, and they come in endless colors.

Small Candy Bits: From Pop Rocks to Nerds, small candies make for perfect toppers, especially for kids. If it's sweet, small, and sugary, let's think of it as a sprinkle in disguise.

Sprinkles for Allergies: India Tree brand specializes in sprinkles colored naturally, using vegetable colorants and other natural ingredients. These come in handy when baking for people with allergies and other dietary restrictions.

Vermicelli Sprinkles: Similarly slender and long like jimmies, these sprinkles are the best quality because they are almost always made from premium chocolate and are available in white, milk, or dark chocolate.

HOMEMADE SPRINKLES

MAKES ABOUT 4 CUPS

Making your very own sprinkles is the best way to customize the color, as well as to achieve the long, slender jimmy shape. And if that isn't exciting enough, you can add shimmer, shine, and flavoring. Since homemade sprinkles are essentially dried royal icing, it's a fun way to use up any icing left over after cookie decorating and fancy cake projects.

1 recipe Royal Icing
(page 194)

AmeriColor gel paste food colors in desired shades

TOOLS
Pastry bags

Couplers

Decorating tips #2

1 Cut eight sheets of wax paper. Fit a pastry bag (or several if you're using a variety of colors) with a #2 round tip. Tint the icing as desired, and then thin the icing slightly by adding about 1 tablespoon water until it reaches a glossy, medium-peak consistency. Fill the pastry bag (no more than half full) with the icing (see page 131 for instructions).

2 Pipe long rows of icing onto the prepared wax paper. Let dry at least 3 hours or overnight.

3 Use a sharp knife to cut the lines of icing into small pieces. Store the sprinkles in plastic zip-top bags or jars indefinitely.

NOTES: For flavored sprinkles, try one of the flavored Royal Icing variations (page 196), or simply add your own flavor of oil or extracts to taste before filling the pastry bags. ⬚ To add shimmer, use a clean, dry, food-safe paintbrush and dust your favorite luster dust onto the dried sprinkles.

WOW FACTOR WITH NOW FACTOR

You can color your own sanding sugar in a snap! That way you can customize the colors any way you wish. Pour about 1 cup white sanding sugar in a bowl, add a drop (or more if you want a more intense shade) of gel paste color, and blend with a rubber spatula. Pour onto a wax paper–lined baking sheet or plate to dry and work any remaining chunks of color in with your hands. Let dry. Store the sugar in an airtight container at room temperature and away from sunlight. If you have the corresponding colors of disco dust, you can add some for extra twinkle.

PINK CHERRY PARTY CUPCAKES

MAKES 12 CUPCAKES

After my not-much-of-a-baker husband made me a cherry chip layer cake during our first week of dating, and then again on our wedding night as a surprise, I have a soft spot for pink cake of any kind. These charming cupcakes are as light and fluffy as can be, and are topped with swirls of sweet and creamy pink cherry frosting. I then toss on an array of pink sprinkles, and top them with bright red Maraschino cherries.

1¾ cups (200 g) cake flour, sifted, plus more for cherries

1 cup plus 2 tablespoons (225 g) superfine sugar

2 teaspoons baking powder

½ teaspoon salt

6 tablespoons (90 g) cold unsalted butter, cut into pieces

¾ cup (180 ml) milk, room temperature

1 tablespoon Maraschino cherry juice

1 teaspoon fresh lemon juice

½ teaspoon pure vanilla extract

4 large egg whites, room temperature

12 (70 g) Maraschino cherries, chopped

1 recipe Vanilla Bakery Frosting (page 180), pink cherry variation

Pink sprinkles

12 Maraschino cherries with stems intact

TOOLS
Cupcake liners

Pastry bag

Decorating tip #1A

1 Preheat the oven to 350°F (180°C). Line a cupcake pan with cupcake liners.

2 In the bowl of an electric mixer fitted with the paddle attachment, combine the flour, sugar, baking powder, and salt on low speed. Add the cold butter one piece at a time. Beat on low speed until all of the butter has been incorporated, about 3 minutes. The mixture should have a fine crumbly, cornmeal-like texture.

3 In a medium measuring cup with a spout, combine half of the milk, the cherry juice, lemon juice, and vanilla. In a separate measuring cup, gently whisk the egg whites and the remaining milk.

4 With the mixer running on medium speed, gradually add the cherry juice mixture and beat for 5 minutes. Scrape the sides and bottom of the bowl with a rubber spatula. Reduce the speed to low, gradually add the egg white mixture, and beat for 1 more minute. Toss the chopped cherries in a little flour, and gently fold them into the batter (be careful not to over-mix). Divide the batter evenly among the cupcake liners.

5 Bake until a wooden pick inserted into the center comes out with a few crumbs, 17 to 20 minutes. Carefully remove the cupcakes from the pan immediately, put them on a wire rack, and let cool completely.

6 Fit a pastry bag with a large round icing tip and fill the bag about two-thirds full with the frosting (see page 131 for instructions). Pipe a generous swirl of frosting on each cupcake. Top each cupcake with a handful of pink sprinkles and a cherry.

7 Store the cupcakes loosely covered at room temperature for up to 2 days.

CONFETTILICIOUS CUPCAKES

MAKES 12 CUPCAKES

These super-fluffy, sprinkle-filled cupcakes are most reminiscent of the boxed Funfetti mixes that so many of us adore, but so much better. You can tint the frosting any shade you like, or keep it creamy white—either way, I suggest keeping it dreamy and light. Of all of the desserts I bake, these cupcakes are the most requested among friends and family, and I think I know why. With a generous swirl of sweet, fluffy Vanilla Bakery Frosting and topped with many a sprinkle, one might say these are happiness in cupcake form.

1¾ cups (200 g) cake flour, sifted

1 cup plus 3 tablespoons (240 g) superfine sugar

2 teaspoons baking powder

½ teaspoon salt

6 tablespoons (90 g) cold unsalted butter, cut into pieces

¾ cup (180 ml) milk, room temperature

1 teaspoon pure vanilla extract or Princess Bakery Emulsion (see Note, page 148)

½ teaspoon fresh lemon juice

4 large egg whites, room temperature

½ cup (75 g) mixture of confetti quins and star quins

1 recipe Vanilla Bakery Frosting (page 180)

AmeriColor gel paste food color in Turquoise

Confetti quin sprinkles

TOOLS
Cupcake liners

Pastry bag

Decorating tip #1A

1 Preheat the oven to 350°F (180°C). Line a cupcake pan with cupcake liners.

2 Into the bowl of an electric mixer fitted with the paddle attachment, sift together the flour, sugar, baking powder, and salt. With the mixer running on low speed, gradually add the butter one piece at a time. Beat until all of the butter has been incorporated, about 3 minutes. The mixture should have a fine crumbly, cornmeal-like texture.

3 In a medium measuring cup with a spout, combine half of the milk, the vanilla, and lemon juice. In a separate measuring cup, gently whisk the egg whites and remaining milk.

4 With the mixer running on medium-low speed, gradually add the vanilla mixture and beat for 5 minutes. Scrape the sides and bottom of the bowl with a rubber spatula. Add the egg white mixture in three parts, scraping down the sides of the bowl after each addition. Reduce the speed to low and beat for 1 more minute. Gently fold in the confetti quin mixture (be careful not to over-mix). The batter will be thin. Fill the cupcake liners two-thirds full.

5 Bake until a wooden pick inserted into the center comes out with a few crumbs, 17 to 20 minutes. Carefully remove the cupcakes from the pan immediately, put them on a wire rack, and let cool completely.

6 Tint the frosting using a few drops of Turquoise color. Fill a pastry bag fitted with a large round tip two-thirds full with frosting (see page 131 for instructions). Pipe a large swirl of frosting on top of each cupcake, toss on the sprinkles, and serve.

7 Store the cupcakes loosely covered at room temperature for up to 2 days.

NOTE: I recommend confetti quins for the batter if you like your sprinkles to stay intact while baking, but nonpareils and jimmies will also work—they will simply leave a bit more of a colorful trail when baked.

SPRINKLE-ME-SILLY PIZZA

MAKES ONE 9-INCH PIZZA

This recipe came to be one day when my little girls were begging me for pizza but I didn't have enough time to create the traditional pizza dough. To be silly, and maybe a bit sassy, I made them this dessert version as a surprise. It's essentially a triple-chocolate sprinkle bark, but with a round pizza shape that's cut into slices. While you can make the base out of any variety of chocolate, I prefer a nice dark chocolate that's not too intense (about 53%). I used milk chocolate chips to create a "crust" and Belgian white chocolate for the "cheese."

10 ounces (290 g) best-quality dark chocolate, chopped or callets/discs (I use Callebaut 53% Dark Chocolate)

1 ounce (30 g) milk chocolate chips or peanut butter chips

¼ cup (30 g) chocolate wafer cookies, broken into small pieces

7 ounces (200 g) best-quality white chocolate, chopped or callets/discs (I use Callebaut)

Sprinkles—every and any kind!

Edible metallic stars

TOOLS

Cake-decorating turntable (optional)

Small offset palette knife

Small sharp knife or pizza cutter

1 Remove the frame of a springform pan and put a piece of wax paper larger than the pan over the base of it and extending over the sides of the pan a few inches. Secure the frame of the pan back in place. Put the pan on a cake-decorating turntable, if using.

2 Temper the dark chocolate (see page 145 for instructions) and pour it into the prepared pan. Using a small offset palette knife, spread the chocolate into an even layer. Sprinkle the milk chocolate chips along the perimeter of the dark chocolate to build a "crust," and use a spoon to cover them with the dark chocolate. Using one hand to rotate the table and the other to hold the palette knife in place against the center surface of the chocolate, smooth the center of the pizza, working outward to the crust.

3 Sprinkle the pizza (but not the crust) evenly with the chocolate cookie pieces. Refrigerate until the chocolate is semi-set, about 4 minutes. Remove the pan from the refrigerator and use the small sharp knife or pizza cutter to gently cut the pizza into 8 slices.

4 Temper the white chocolate (see page 145 for instructions) and spread it across the dark chocolate using a clean small offset palette knife, leaving the crust exposed. Cover the white chocolate with a generous array of sprinkles and stars. Refrigerate until the white chocolate partially sets, about 5 minutes. Slice the pizza again, using the existing slices as a guide. Let the pizza sit at room temperature until set, about 1 hour.

5 Carefully remove the outer ring of the springform pan. Use a knife to separate the slices, and serve.

6 Store in an airtight container in a cool, dry place away from sunlight for up to 2 weeks.

NOTES: Because you've tempered the chocolate, it will keep its gorgeous shine and snap even at room temperature, which makes the pizza perfect for gifting or for giving as party favors. Simply wrap individual slices in clear cellophane and tie with a fun, colorful ribbon. ◼ When it comes to the pizza "toppings," you don't need to stick to sprinkles, per se—I've been known to toss jelly beans, Pop Rocks, or pretty much any other tasty confection on this pizza. Have fun with it!

cakelets
IN THE KITCHEN

Let kids go sprinkle-crazy by allowing them to do the tossing. Give them cupcake liners filled with every sprinkle you've got, and let them go wild. Just have them work fast, as the chocolate sets up quickly.

These sparkly stars are edible!

SKY-HIGH CHOCOLATE-COVERED CUPCAKES

MAKES ABOUT 18 CUPCAKES

I believe that sometimes sprinkles and sparkles can be subtle and still work the same magic—especially when they are perched atop a towering mound of dreamy marshmallow frosting covered in rich chocolate glaze and nestled on a deep, dark, moist chocolate cupcake. The generous sprinkling of rainbow nonpareils and shimmery stars topped with a bright pink gumball makes these otherwise old-fashioned cupcakes simple but sprinkletastic.

1¼ cups (160 g) all-purpose flour

½ cup (60 g) Dutch-process dark cocoa powder (I like Cacao Barry Extra Brute)

2 teaspoons baking soda

¾ teaspoon baking powder

½ teaspoon salt

1¼ cups (260 g) superfine sugar

¾ cup (180 ml) buttermilk, room temperature

¾ cup (180 ml) hot coffee or espresso

⅓ cup (80 ml) vegetable oil

1 large egg, room temperature

1 teaspoon pure vanilla extract

2 recipes Marshmallow Frosting (page 173)

2 recipes Shiny Chocolate Glaze (page 188)

Rainbow nonpareils

Edible metallic stars

Gumballs

TOOLS

Cupcake liners

Pastry bag

Decorating tip #1A

1 Preheat the oven to 350°F (180°C). Line two cupcake pans with 18 cupcake liners.

2 Into the bowl of an electric mixer fitted with the whisk attachment, sift the flour, cocoa powder, baking soda, baking powder, and salt. Add the sugar and whisk to combine.

3 In a large measuring cup with a spout, whisk together the buttermilk, coffee, oil, egg, and vanilla. With the mixer running on low speed, gradually add the milk mixture and beat until smooth. Use a rubber spatula to scrape the sides and bottom of the bowl. Divide the batter among the cupcake liners.

4 Bake until a wooden pick inserted into the center comes out with a few crumbs, 18 to 20 minutes. Carefully remove the cupcakes from the pan immediately, put them on a wire rack, and let cool completely.

5 Fill a large pastry bag fitted with a large round tip two-thirds full with the marshmallow frosting (see page 131 for instructions). Working in a circular motion from the inside, out and up, pipe a big swirl atop each cupcake. Set the filled pastry bag aside. Refrigerate until the frosting firms up slightly, about 30 minutes.

6 Remove the cupcakes from the refrigerator and spoon the chocolate glaze over the frosting. Sprinkle with a generous coating of rainbow nonpareils and metallic stars. Use the reserved filled pastry bag to add a small swirl of marshmallow frosting to the top of each cupcake. Top with a gumball, and serve.

7 The cupcakes will keep loosely covered at room temperature for up to 2 days.

SPRINKLE-DIPPED MERINGUES

MAKES ABOUT
30 COOKIES

I can think of only one thing that makes crispy, melt-in-your-mouth poofs of light, heavenly meringue even better: sprinkles. The bottoms of these pure white cookies are dipped in creamy white chocolate and coated in a medley of sprinkles, giving them a super-celebratory feel. And while these treats would look super-pretty in any shade of pastel, there's something about the contrast of the pure white against the vibrant sprinkles-and-such that really makes them pop.

---

3 large egg whites, room temperature

Pinch of cream of tartar

¾ cup (155 g) superfine sugar

1 teaspoon pure vanilla or almond extract

3 ounces (90 g) best-quality white chocolate, chopped or callets/discs (I like Callebaut)

Sprinkles of your choice

TOOLS
Large pastry bag
Decorating tip #1A

NOTE: When making meringue, be sure that your mixer bowl and whisk are completely free from even a smidge of grease or other residue. For the most stable and voluminous meringue, I find it's best to use fresh eggs, without a trace of yolk, and not pre-packaged egg whites. Egg whites tend to separate best when they are cold, but they whip up best when room temperature or warm.

1 Preheat the oven to 200°F (90°C). Line two baking sheets with parchment and set aside.

2 Wipe a stainless steel bowl and the whisk of an electric mixer with a paper towel dampened with a little lemon juice to eliminate any trace of grease. Put the egg whites into the bowl and beat on low speed until foamy, about 30 seconds. Stop the mixer and add the cream of tartar. Increase the speed to medium and beat until soft peaks form, about 1 minute. Increase the speed to medium-high and add the sugar one spoonful at a time. Beat on high speed until very stiff peaks form and the meringue is glossy and thick, about 3 minutes. Add the vanilla and beat for 1 more minute.

3 Fit a large pastry bag with a large round decorating tip and pipe 2-inch-diameter cookies about 1 inch apart onto the prepared baking sheets.

4 Bake in the upper and lower third of the oven for 1½ hours undisturbed, and then turn off the oven. Leave the cookies inside the oven for 1 more hour to dry out. The cookies should be crisp, but not browned or discolored. Transfer the baking sheets to wire racks to cool completely.

5 In a heatproof bowl, melt the white chocolate either in the microwave in 20-second intervals (be careful not to burn it) or over a small saucepan of simmering water. Line two baking sheets with fresh parchment paper and fill a shallow dish with the sprinkles. Dip the bottom of each meringue into the white chocolate, and then immediately dip them into the sprinkles. Put them on the prepared baking sheets and let them set, about 1 hour.

6 The meringues will keep in an airtight container at room temperature for up to 5 days.

VARIATIONS

- **Cotton Candy Sprinkle Meringues:** Replace the sugar with cotton candy sugar.

- **Dark Chocolate–Dipped Meringues:** Replace the white chocolate with dark chocolate. You could even use all chocolate vermicelli sprinkles in place of the rainbow sprinkles.

- **Double-Sprinkle Meringues:** Fold ½ cup of your favorite sprinkles into the meringue before piping.

- **Sparkly Sprinkle Meringues:** Dip the meringues in a glittering medley of metallic sprinkles and sanding sugar—you can even sprinkle with a hit of glitter before baking for a subtle sparkle.

RED VELVET CAKELETS

MAKES 12 CAKELETS

These decadent cakelets are fancy and fabulous. Moist red velvet cakelets are baked in a jumbo muffin pan and are covered in a generous swirl of fluffy cream cheese frosting, encrusted in heart sprinkles, and topped with a ruby-slipper-inspired glittered cherry for an extra dose of dazzle.

1 recipe **Red Velvet Cake batter** (page 157)

Piping jelly

12 fresh cherries with stems intact

Red disco dust

1 recipe **Fluffy Cream Cheese Frosting** (page 183)

Medley of red, pink, and white heart sprinkles

TOOLS
Jumbo cupcake liners

Small food-safe paintbrush

Pastry bag

Decorating tip #1A (or other large round tip)

1 Preheat the oven to 350°F (180°C). Line a jumbo cupcake pan with liners.

2 Fill each cupcake liner with about ⅔ cup batter. Bake until a wooden pick inserted into the center comes out with a few crumbs, 22 to 24 minutes. Carefully transfer the cupcakes from the pan onto a wire rack and let cool completely.

3 Paint a thin layer of piping jelly onto each cherry (not the stem) and sprinkle with disco dust. Set aside.

4 Fit your pastry bag with a large round icing tip and fill the bag about two-thirds full with the frosting (see page 131 for instructions). Pipe a generous swirl of frosting on each cupcake.

5 Put the sprinkle mixture on a small plate. Hold the frosted cakelets sideways over the plate and gently press the sprinkles into the edges of the frosting, going all the way around. Top each cakelet with a glittered cherry.

6 The cakelets will keep loosely covered at cool room temperature for up to 24 hours, or in the refrigerator for up to 2 days.

BIRTHDAY CAKE LOLLIPOPS

MAKES 6 LOLLIPOPS

Just when we thought lollipops were already all sunshine and, well, lollipops, we're going to make them taste just like vanilla birthday cake, color them stark white, and cover them with sprinkles. After experimenting with nearly every flavor of candy oil on the market, I've concluded that "cheesecake" flavor adds the most birthday cake–like taste. Wrap these cuties individually in cellophane, tie with a polka-dot bow, and give them as a party favor or gift, or keep them in your handbag for an emergency birthday cake fix.

Confetti quin sprinkles

Star quin sprinkles

¼ cup (85 g) light corn syrup (see Note, page 42)

¼ cup (60 ml) water

1¼ cups (250 g) granulated sugar

Pinch of salt

1 tablespoon AmeriColor gel paste food color in Bright White

½ teaspoon cheesecake-flavor oil (I use LorAnn Oils brand)

TOOLS

2 medium lollipop molds (three 2½-inch cavities per mold)

Nonstick cooking spray

Six 4-inch lollipop sticks

Tape (such as masking tape)

Pastry brush

Candy thermometer

1 Lightly grease the lollipop molds by lightly spraying a paper towel with cooking spray and coating each round cavity. Spray a measuring cup with the cooking spray and set it beside the stovetop. Generously sprinkle each lollipop mold with confetti and star quins. Put the lollipop sticks into the designated "stick spots" on the molds, extending the sticks about ¾ inch into each round cavity. Tape each stick in place. Set aside.

2 In a small saucepan set over medium heat, cook the corn syrup, water, sugar, and salt until the sugar has dissolved, about 1 minute. Brush the sides of the saucepan with a damp pastry brush and clip on a candy thermometer. Increase the heat to high and boil the mixture, undisturbed, until the candy thermometer reads 240°F (115°C), about 5 minutes. Add the white gel paste food color, but don't stir. Let the syrup boil undisturbed until it reaches 300°F (150°C), about 3 more minutes.

3 Promptly remove the pan from the heat and quickly (and carefully) pour the mixture into a spouted measuring cup. Using a heatproof spatula, stir in the cheesecake oil until some of the air bubbles have settled. Work quickly, as the sugar sets up almost immediately. Carefully fill two lollipop molds and sprinkle the tops with more quins and stars (the tops harden almost immediately). Repeat with the remaining lollipop molds. Let cool at room temperature for 1 to 2 hours.

4 Remove the lollipops from the mold by gently twisting the mold and lifting by the sticks.

5 The lollipops will keep in an airtight container at room temperature for up to 2 weeks.

CONEY ISLAND CHEESECAKE

MAKES ONE 9-INCH ROUND CHEESECAKE (14 SERVINGS)

Here, I've taken a classic baked cheesecake and added some carnival style. Rich, creamy confetti-flecked cheesecake is baked into a buttery crumb crust made with a combination of animal crackers, sugar cones, and peanuts, all topped with a pastel blue and pink cotton candy whipped cream and more sprinkles. This is one seriously velvety and gloriously smooth and dense baked cheesecake, and it can be easily modified to represent a more traditional baked cheesecake.

CRUST

2 cups (130 g) store-bought animal crackers

2 standard waffle cones or sugar cones (40 g)

2 tablespoons salted roasted peanuts

2 tablespoons granulated sugar

1 teaspoon dry milk powder

½ teaspoon sea salt

6 tablespoons (90 g) unsalted butter, melted

FILLING

5 (8-oz/225 g) packages cream cheese, room temperature and cut into pieces

1¼ cups (260 g) superfine sugar

2 tablespoons all-purpose flour

½ cup (115 g) sour cream, room temperature

¼ cup (60 ml) vanilla ice cream, melted

1 tablespoon Princess Bakery Emulsion (see Note, page 148) or pure vanilla extract

Pinch of salt

5 large eggs, room temperature

½ cup (75 g) confetti quin sprinkles, plus more for decorating

1. Fill a roasting pan with about 1 inch of warm water and put it in the oven on the center rack. Preheat the oven to 325°F (165°C). Grease a 9-inch springform pan with cooking spray and line the bottom with parchment.

2. For the crust: In a food processor, pulse together the animal crackers, waffle cones, peanuts, sugar, dry milk, and salt until they become coarse crumbs. Add the butter and pulse to combine. Press the mixture into the bottom of the prepared springform pan, coming up the sides about 1 inch all around. Set aside.

3. For the filling: In the bowl of an electric mixer fitted with the paddle attachment, beat the cream cheese on medium speed until smooth, about 2 minutes (do not over-beat). Add the sugar, flour, sour cream, ice cream, emulsion, and salt and beat for about 1 minute. Reduce the speed to low and add the eggs, one at a time, mixing for 30 seconds after each addition. Use a rubber spatula to scrape the sides and bottom of the bowl. Strain the batter into a large bowl, using a rubber spatula to help push it through the sieve. Fold in the confetti quins.

4. Pour the filling into the crust. Slide the cheesecake into the oven bag and secure the top of the bag loosely. Put the bag with the cheesecake into the roasting pan of hot water, and put the pan into the oven.

5. Bake for 1 hour. Turn off the oven and let the cheesecake sit in the oven until the center reaches 150°–155°F, about 20 minutes. Remove the cheesecake from the roasting pan, discard the oven bag, and run a small knife around the edges of the crust. Let cool completely on a wire rack. Refrigerate for at least 8 hours.

6. For the whipped cream: Put the stainless steel mixer bowl and whisk in the freezer for at least 15 minutes. Beat the cream, sugar,

COTTON CANDY WHIPPED CREAM

1 cup (240 ml) whipping cream, cold

2 tablespoons superfine sugar

¼ teaspoon cotton candy oil (I use LorAnn Oils)

Drop of AmeriColor gel paste food color in Sky Blue and Soft Pink (or other desired colors)

TOOLS

Nonstick cooking spray

1 oven bag (see Note)

2 pastry bags

2 decorating tips #1E

Digital thermometer

NOTE: I prefer using an oven bag—the ones typically used for cooking a turkey—as opposed to foil because it guarantees that no water from the water bath leaks in from the bottom of the pan.

and cotton candy oil on medium speed until stiff peaks form, about 1 minute. Divide the whipped cream evenly between two medium bowls and tint one half pastel blue and other half pastel pink. Keep covered and chilled until ready to use.

7 Carefully remove the outer ring of the springform pan and transfer the cheesecake to a serving platter or plate. When ready to serve the cheesecake, fit each pastry bag with the decorating tip and fill each bag with the colored whipped cream. Pipe large stars on top of the cheesecake, alternating between pink and blue. Sprinkle a generous handful of quins on top, and serve.

8 The cheesecake will keep in the refrigerator for up to 1 week.

NOTE: For a flawless cheesecake, be sure to use room-temperature ingredients, do not over-mix, and do not over-bake. Straining the batter can be a little messy, but it makes for an even more velvety texture. A water bath is a must for adding moisture to the oven, which results in a gloriously smooth cheesecake.

VARIATION

- **Classic New York Cheesecake:** Replace the carnival crust with 2½ cups (215 g) graham cracker crumbs mixed with ½ cup (115 g) melted unsalted butter and 2 tablespoons granulated sugar. Add 2 teaspoons lemon juice to the filling and omit the sprinkles and cotton candy whipped cream.

RAINBOWS & SPRINKLES CAKE

MAKES ONE 6-LAYER CAKE (12 TO 14 SERVINGS)

I heart sprinkles. I just do. You can use a mix of any of your favorite store-bought sprinkles, or you can even make your own (see page 16) for a customized creation.

1 recipe Super White Cake batter (page 148)

AmeriColor gel paste food color in Electric Blue, Electric Green, Electric Orange, Electric Purple, Soft Pink, and Turquoise

1 recipe Swiss Meringue Buttercream (page 176)

3 cups (450 g) mixed sprinkles

TOOLS

8-inch round thin cake board (optional)

Cake-decorating turntable (optional)

Pastry brush

Small offset palette knife

Pastry bag

Decorating tip #887

1 Preheat the oven to 350°F (180°C). Grease the bottoms of two 8 × 2-inch round cake pans and line with parchment.

2 Divide the batter among six small bowls. Tint each bowl of batter using a few drops each of Electric Blue, Electric Green, Electric Orange, Electric Purple, Soft Pink, and Turquoise gel paste color. Pour two of the tinted batters separately into the two prepared cake pans (each layer will be pancake-thin). Bake in the center of the oven until a wooden pick inserted in the center comes out with a few crumbs, 10 to 12 minutes. Repeat with the remaining batter. Let the cakes cool in the pans on wire racks for 10 minutes. Run a knife around the edges, and carefully turn the layers out onto wire racks. Peel off the paper, and let cool completely.

3 Put a cake board or cake plate on a cake-decorating turntable, if using, and put the purple cake layer, top up, on the board. Brush away any stray crumbs using a dry pastry brush.

4 Using a small offset palette knife, spread about ¼ cup of the buttercream on the top of the purple layer. Place the blue cake layer on top, top up, and repeat to add the green, pink, and orange layers. Put the teal layer on top, bottom up.

5 Tint the remaining buttercream using a few drops of Turquoise color. Frost the entire cake with the turquoise buttercream (see page 135 for instructions). Refrigerate the cake for 15 minutes.

6 Fit a pastry bag with the decorating tip and fill it two-thirds full of the turquoise buttercream (see page 131 for instructions).

7 Put the mixed sprinkles into a large bowl. Holding the cake over the bowl, gently press the sprinkles all over the sides of the cake, working from the top down. Return the cake to the turntable and pipe a large buttercream border around the perimeter of the top of the cake. Refrigerate for 15 minutes.

8 The cake will keep at room temperature for up to 8 hours, and then in the refrigerator for up to 3 days.

For a super-duper sprinkly good time, let kids help "throw" the sprinkles on the cake (just be sure to keep a baking sheet under the large bowl of sprinkles first, or it will be a rainbow sprinkle rainstorm all over the kitchen!).

WONDROUS
SWEETS FOR THE WEE

PAINTED MINI CAKES

· · · · · · · · · · · · · ·

SPARKLY FLOWER
COOKIE POPS

· · · · · · · · · · · · · ·

CANDY BIRTHSTONE GEMS

· · · · · · · · · · · · · ·

BIRTHDAY CAKE
MILKSHAKES

· · · · · · · · · · · · · ·

WEE LITTLE CHOCOLATE
CUPCAKES

· · · · · · · · · · · · · ·

POP ROCK ROBOTS

· · · · · · · · · · · · · ·

PINK CANDIED CARNIVAL
POPCORN

· · · · · · · · · · · · · ·

COTTON CANDY CUPCAKES

· · · · · · · · · · · · · ·

CHALK-A-LOT COOKIES
WITH EDIBLE CHALK

· · · · · · · · · · · · · ·

CUT & PASTE
ILLUSTRATION CAKE

· · · · · · · · · · · · · ·

RAINBOW DOODLE
COOKIES

· · · · · · · · · · · · · ·

PAINTED MINI CAKES

MAKES FOUR 4-INCH ROUND CAKES

So perhaps this chapter should be entitled "Wondrous Desserts for the Wee at Heart," because I think we all secretly crave rainbows and craft time. This is one of my girls' most loved desserts, and I'm sure you can imagine why. Sweet-as-can-be, personal-size chocolate cakes filled with meringue buttercream and covered in pure white fondant are just waiting to be painted upon. Maybe it's because kids are so accustomed to not eating paint that they revel in this idea.

1 recipe Simple & Splendid Chocolate Cake batter (page 152)

1 recipe Swiss Meringue Buttercream (page 176) or Italian Meringue Buttercream (page 174), flavored as desired

3 pounds (1¼ kg) white ready-to-use fondant

AmeriColor gel paste food color in desired shades

TOOLS

4-inch pastry ring

4 round thin 4-inch cake boards

Artist's paint palette or as many ramekins as you have gel colors

Clear lemon extract

Food-safe paintbrushes

1 Preheat the oven to 350°F (180°C). Grease the bottom of a baker's half-sheet pan (13 × 18 × 1 inch) and line the bottom with parchment.

2 Pour the cake batter into the prepared pan. Bake until a wooden pick inserted in the center comes out with a few crumbs, 18 to 22 minutes. Let cool completely in the pan. Cover the pan with plastic wrap and refrigerate for at least 1 hour.

3 Using a 4-inch pastry ring, cut out 12 circles of cake from the sheet cake. Make four 3-layer cakes by filling and frosting the circles, putting each on a 4-inch cake board (see page 135 for instructions). Refrigerate until the buttercream is very firm, at least 1 hour.

4 Cover each cake with white fondant, using 12 ounces (340 g) of the fondant per cake (see page 139 for instructions). Refrigerate until firm, at least 1 hour. If the cakes get sticky after you've removed them from the refrigerator, let them sit for about 30 minutes (or if you're in a rush, you can always use a fan to dry the cake "sweat").

5 Set up the painting station: Squeeze each gel paste color onto the paint palette and dilute with clear lemon extract for less concentrated colors, mixing with a paintbrush. Set each child up with his or her own wax paper mat, paper towel, paint, brushes, and cake. The edible paint dries very quickly, so you will need to let it dry for only about 30 minutes before serving.

6 These cakes will keep at cool room temperature for up to 24 hours, and then refrigerated for up to 3 days.

NOTE: If the kids want to get really creative, try giving them tissues, sponges, or any fun (and clean) item around the house to create textures.

SPARKLY FLOWER COOKIE POPS

MAKES 12 LARGE COOKIE POPS

I may not be known for my green thumb, but I can grow these adorable cookie flowers. These happy, big-as-can-be cookies are simple to make and easy for kids to help decorate. Reese and Neve love to get right in there and cover the cookies with the brightest sanding sugar possible before choosing their own finishing touches, like gumballs and even little candy bees. We've made them into cookie pops, because who doesn't love eating sweets on a stick? While I've made this batch turquoise, you really can't go wrong with other colors—the brighter, the better, we say.

---

1 recipe Vanilla Sugar Cutout Cookies dough (page 163), flavored as desired, chilled

2 recipes Royal Icing (page 194)

AmeriColor gel paste food color in Turquoise

2 cups sanding sugar colored turquoise (see page 16)

12 large gumballs

TOOLS

5-inch-wide flower cookie cutter

Twelve 8-inch cookie sticks (I use Wilton brand)

Pastry bag

Coupler

Decorating tip #3

12 green striped paper straws (optional)

1 Roll out and chill the cookie dough according to the recipe (see page 163). Cut out 12 large flower cookies. Insert a cookie stick into the base of each cookie, gently twisting while pushing the stick about 1½ inches inside the cookie. Carefully transfer the cookies to baking sheets and chill the cookies according to the recipe.

2 Preheat the oven to 350°F (180°C). Bake the cookies according to the recipe and let cool completely.

3 Tint the royal icing turquoise with the gel paste, and then stir in a few drops of water to achieve the 10-second consistency (see page 194 for instructions). Fill a pastry bag fitted with a coupler and small round decorating tip one-half full with the turquoise icing (see page 131 for instructions). Keep the tip of the pastry bag covered with a damp cloth when not in use.

4 Put a piece of wax paper on a baking sheet and put the turquoise sanding sugar in a small bowl. Outline and fill 1 cookie with the turquoise icing (see page 133 for instructions), and put a gumball in the center. Transfer the cookie to the prepared baking sheet and cover the wet icing with the sanding sugar. (You will shake off the excess once the icing has dried and the gumball is in place.) Repeat with the remaining cookies. Let dry for at least 2 hours. Reserve the remaining icing.

5 Gently shake off the excess sanding sugar from the dry cookies back onto the wax paper and return the sugar to its container. Let the cookies dry for 12 to 24 hours.

6 Slide a green paper straw (if using) over each cookie stick to create a stem.

7 The cookies will keep in an airtight container for up to 1 week.

cakelets
IN THE KITCHEN *These cookies are perfect for kids to help decorate—let them add the gumballs, toss the sugar over the cookies, or even choose their own color scheme. Since you've got the baking sheet set up underneath, cleanup is quick and easy!*

CANDY BIRTHSTONE GEMS

MAKES ABOUT 24 GEMS

My little girls have recently discovered their birthstones—and who knew they'd find such a thing so fascinating? I thought it would be pretty neat to tailor batches of hard candy gems using the colors of their birthstones, and they thought this was the best thing ever. And for some reason I find making hard candy at home feels so official, like I've accomplished something extraordinary. If you haven't used a candy thermometer before, don't be intimidated—it's so much easier than it sounds. While these darling gems are delightful all on their own, you can also try perching them atop yummy cupcakes or using them as cake decorations.

1¼ cups (250 g) granulated sugar

¼ cup (85 g) light corn syrup (see Note)

¼ cup (60 ml) water

AmeriColor gel paste food color of choice (see Chart)

Pinch of salt

½ teaspoon flavor oil of choice (I use LorAnn Oils)

TOOLS

Large and medium gem hard candy molds

Nonstick cooking spray

Pastry brush

Candy thermometer

1　Lightly coat the gem molds with cooking spray and put them aside on wax paper. Coat a small, heatproof measuring cup with a spout with cooking spray and put it beside the stovetop.

2　In a medium saucepan set over medium heat, cook the sugar, corn syrup, water, gel paste, and salt until the sugar has dissolved, about 3 minutes. Brush down the sides of the saucepan with a damp pastry brush and clip on a candy thermometer. Increase the heat to high and boil, undisturbed, until the candy thermometer reads 295°F (146°C). Promptly remove the pan from the heat and quickly (and carefully) transfer the candy to the prepared measuring cup. Using a heatproof spatula, quickly stir in the flavor oil until some of the bubbles have settled. Work quickly, as the sugar sets up almost immediately.

3　Carefully fill each gem mold and let the trays cool completely at room temperature, about 1 hour. Remove the candies by gently twisting the molds.

4　The candies will keep in an airtight container at room temperature for up to 2 weeks.

NOTE: When hard candy is exposed to air for an extended period of time, it can become sticky. For a less sticky version, use LorAnn Oils Hi-Sweet product (see Sources, page 203)—a powdered corn syrup replacement that helps keep hard candy from getting sticky—instead of regular corn syrup. ◾ To give these gems even more shine, buff the cooled candies with a small amount of cooking oil and a paper towel.

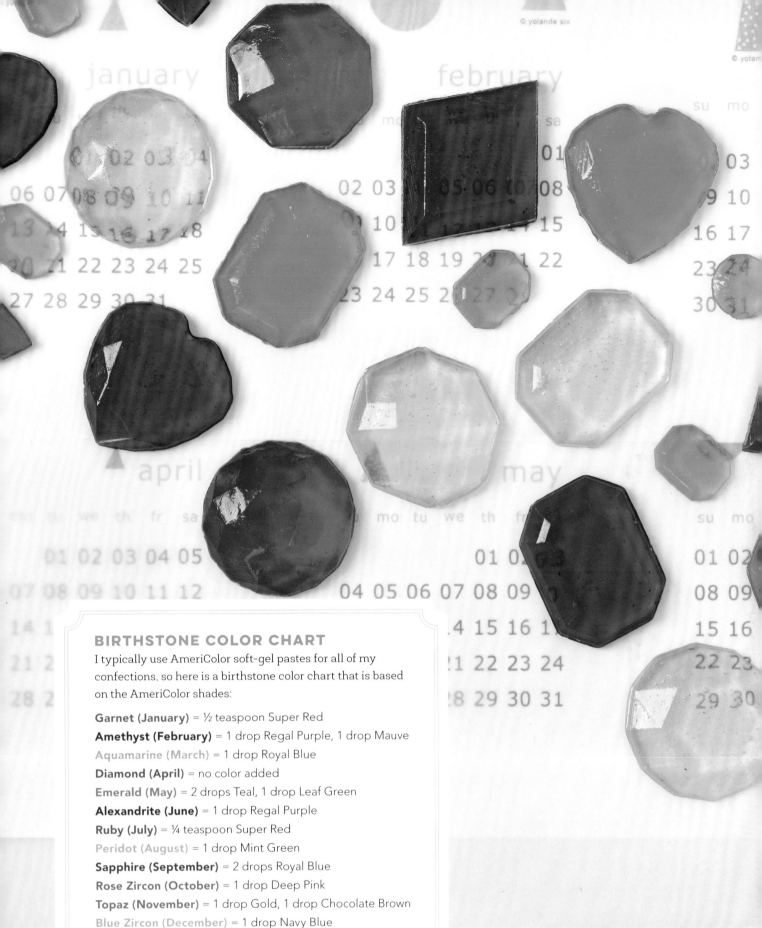

BIRTHSTONE COLOR CHART

I typically use AmeriColor soft-gel pastes for all of my confections, so here is a birthstone color chart that is based on the AmeriColor shades:

Garnet (January) = ½ teaspoon Super Red

Amethyst (February) = 1 drop Regal Purple, 1 drop Mauve

Aquamarine (March) = 1 drop Royal Blue

Diamond (April) = no color added

Emerald (May) = 2 drops Teal, 1 drop Leaf Green

Alexandrite (June) = 1 drop Regal Purple

Ruby (July) = ¼ teaspoon Super Red

Peridot (August) = 1 drop Mint Green

Sapphire (September) = 2 drops Royal Blue

Rose Zircon (October) = 1 drop Deep Pink

Topaz (November) = 1 drop Gold, 1 drop Chocolate Brown

Blue Zircon (December) = 1 drop Navy Blue

BIRTHDAY CAKE MILKSHAKES

MAKES 6 MINI MILKSHAKES

I love making milkshakes for kids because they are so quick and easy—it's like whipping up a birthday party in minutes. When it comes to authentic birthday cake flavor, you don't need store-bought cake mix, since it's actually the store-bought *vanilla frosting* that triggers the memories. The frosting is also the perfect "glue" to adhere the sprinkles to the glasses. The key to a seriously decadent and successful milkshake of any kind, aside from using the best ice cream you can find, is to keep all of your ingredients and equipment chilled up until the very last minute.

Sprinkles

¼ cup (50 g) store-bought vanilla frosting, plus more for glasses

½ cup (120 ml) cold milk

6 scoops (3 cups/720 ml) best-quality vanilla ice cream

Pinch of salt

1 Chill your milkshake glasses in the freezer for at least 30 minutes. Put a few handfuls of sprinkles onto a small plate and a few tablespoons of frosting onto a separate small plate.

2 Remove the glasses from the freezer and dip the rim of each glass into the frosting, followed by the sprinkles. Set aside.

3 In a blender, combine the milk, the ¼ cup frosting, the ice cream, and salt and process until the ingredients are incorporated and you have a thick milkshake. Serve in the prepared glasses.

WEE LITTLE CHOCOLATE CUPCAKES

MAKES ABOUT 52 BITE-SIZE CUPCAKES

Yay for teeny, tiny treats! If there's one thing I've discovered, it's that little things make a whole lotta happy. These super-chocolaty cupcakes, topped with a dollop of decadent glossy fudge frosting and sprinkles, are perfect for wee hands. They are ideal for tea with Teddy or even a full-on birthday extravaganza, where, in my little Reese's perfect world, these would be the only item on the menu. (See photograph on page 36.)

1 recipe Sky-High Chocolate-Dipped Cupcakes batter (page 25)

1 recipe Glossy Fudge Frosting (page 187)

Sprinkles

TOOLS

Mini cupcake liners

Plastic squeeze bottle with wide opening (see Notes)

Pastry bag

Decorating tip #1A

Tiny flag cupcake toppers (optional)

1 Preheat the oven to 350°F (180°C). Line two mini cupcake pans with mini cupcake liners.

2 Fill a plastic squeeze bottle with the batter, and fill each cupcake liner three-fourths full.

3 Bake until a wooden pick inserted into the center comes out with a few crumbs, 6 to 9 minutes. Carefully remove the cupcakes from the pan immediately, put them on a wire rack, and let cool completely.

4 Fill a pastry bag fitted with a large round decorating tip half full with frosting (see page 131 for instructions). Pipe a generous swirl of frosting on top of each cupcake and top with sprinkles. Insert a flag cupcake topper into each cupcake, if desired.

5 The cupcakes will keep loosely covered at room temperature for up to 3 days.

NOTES: The one thing about making mini cupcakes with a thin batter, such as this one, is that it's easy to get more around the cupcake liners than actually in them. A plastic squeeze bottle is a great tool for filling the liners without any mess. ▪ Okay, here's the thing about piping chocolate frosting with a round tip: if you do the classic swirl, it has a way of looking like doggy you-know-what. The secret is this: after frosting the cupcakes, use the back of a small spoon to gently push a little nest at the top, which changes the shape and also holds plenty 'a sprinkles. Just puttin' that out there.

POP ROCK ROBOTS

MAKES ABOUT 24 ROBOTS

These adorable little metallic chocolate robots are filled with snapping, crackling Pop Rocks and given a quick coat of metallic edible paint spray for an authentic metal finish. Why not pass these little charmers around at your next party, just for fun? And while any shape of chocolate mold would work well, there's something about a robot with a belly full of popping candy that makes my cakelets giggle.

7 ounces (200 g) best-quality dark or milk chocolate, chopped or callets/discs (I use Callebaut 53% cacao)

8 packets (about 75 g) Pop Rocks

TOOLS

Food-safe paintbrush

2 robot silicone chocolate molds

Small offset palette knife

Silver edible paint spray (I use Duff's Cake Graffiti in silver)

1 Temper the chocolate (see page 145 for instructions). Using the paintbrush, paint a thin layer of chocolate into each mold cavity. Refrigerate to set, 3 to 5 minutes.

2 Remove the molds from the refrigerator and fill each cavity with Pop Rocks. Pour chocolate in to fill the molds, taking care to not over-fill. Using a palette knife, level the top. Let sit at room temperature to set, about 1 hour.

3 Push the robots out of the molds and put them on a piece of wax paper. Spray the robots with silver spray. Let dry, and then spray with a second coat. Let dry overnight.

4 The robots will keep in a plastic zip-top bag in a cool, dry place away from the sun for up to 2 weeks.

VARIATION

◄ **Cotton Candy Popcorn:**
Replace the sugar with
cotton candy sugar and
increase the water to
⅓ cup (80 ml). Omit the
flavor, extracts, and color,
as the cotton candy sugar
will add both the cotton
candy flavor and color.

PINK CANDIED CARNIVAL POPCORN

MAKES 7 CUPS

While sweet, crunchy candied popcorn is loved across North America in all its variations, this version comes from my Canadian childhood. Lucky Elephant is a Canadian brand of pink candy-coated popcorn that has been around since the 1950s. It is sold in a small box with a tiny prize (like Cracker Jack), and is found only at certain candy shops and small grocers, making it even more desirable. Aside from its highly addictive and distinct, almost fruity taste, it flaunts an iconic coral-pink shade. I've tailored the recipe to celebrate that particular shade of "Lucky Elephant" pink, but of course you can create any shade you wish. Either way, prepare to become addicted.

7 cups popped corn, lightly salted

½ teaspoon clear imitation vanilla extract

½ teaspoon pure almond extract

¼ teaspoon strawberry flavor oil (I use LorAnn Oils)

1¼ cups (250 g) granulated sugar

¼ cup (85 g) light corn syrup

¼ cup (60 ml) water

Pinch of salt

1 tablespoon unsalted butter

3 drops AmeriColor gel paste food color in Soft Pink

1 drop AmeriColor gel paste food color in Electric Yellow

TOOLS

Nonstick cooking spray

Pastry brush

Candy thermometer

1 Preheat the oven to 200°F (90°C). Line a baking sheet with a silicone baking mat or aluminum foil.

2 Lightly coat the inside of a large stainless steel bowl and two wooden spoons with cooking spray. Pour the popcorn into the bowl and put the bowl in the preheated oven while you make the candy coating. In a small dish or ramekin, combine the vanilla and almond extracts and the strawberry flavor oil. Set aside.

3 In a medium saucepan set over medium heat, cook the sugar, corn syrup, water, and salt until the sugar has dissolved, about 1 minute. Brush down the sides of the saucepan with a damp pastry brush and clip on a candy thermometer. Stop stirring. Increase the heat to medium-high and boil, undisturbed, until the candy thermometer reads 240°F (116°C), about 5 minutes. Remove the pan from the heat and add the butter and gel paste colors (no need to stir). Return the pan to the stove and increase the heat to high. Let the syrup boil until it reaches 300°F (150°C), about 3 minutes. While the syrup is boiling, transfer the bowl of warm popcorn to the countertop beside the prepared baking sheet.

4 Remove the pan from the heat and quickly (and carefully) stir in the extract mixture. Working quickly, as the sugar will start to set up almost immediately, pour the syrup in a thin stream all over the popcorn. Using your greased wooden spoons, quickly toss the popcorn to coat each piece with candy. Turn the popcorn out onto the prepared baking sheet and spread it in an even layer. As the candied corn begins to set, carefully break apart any large clumps and separate as many pieces as possible. Let cool completely, about 30 minutes.

5 The popcorn will keep in an airtight container for up to 2 weeks.

COTTON CANDY CUPCAKES

MAKES 20 CUPCAKES

There are few things in this world as magical as cotton candy. Aside from its ethereal and cloud-like pastel appearance, and its melt-in-your-mouth texture, I think one of the reasons children go bonkers for it is that it's typically a once-a-year—or maybe even once-in-a-childhood—experience. These pretty little cakes celebrate cotton candy in all its glory. My girls and I decided that if we could bake a cupcake for our beloved Katy Perry, this would be it.

1¾ cups (200 g) cake flour, sifted

1 cup plus 3 tablespoons (240 g) superfine sugar

2 teaspoons baking powder

½ teaspoon salt

6 tablespoons (90 g) cold unsalted butter, cut into pieces

¾ cup (180 ml) milk, room temperature

¾ teaspoon cotton candy flavor oil (I like LorAnn Oils)

4 large egg whites, room temperature

Few drops AmeriColor gel paste food color in Electric Blue

2 recipes Marshmallow Frosting (page 173), cotton candy variation in 2 different desired flavors

Cotton candy

Edible stars

TOOLS
Cupcake liners
2 pastry bags
Decorating tips #1A and #887

1 Preheat the oven to 350°F (180°C). Line two cupcake pans with 20 cupcake liners.

2 Into the bowl of an electric mixer fitted with the paddle attachment, sift together the flour, sugar, baking powder, and salt. Turn the mixer on low speed and gradually add the butter one piece at a time. Mix until all of the butter has been incorporated, about 3 minutes. The mixture should have a fine crumbly, cornmeal-like texture.

3 In a medium measuring cup with a spout, combine half the milk and the flavor oil. In a separate medium measuring cup, gently whisk the egg whites and remaining milk.

4 Increase the mixer speed to medium-low, gradually add the milk mixture, flavor oil, and color and beat for 5 minutes. Scrape the sides and bottom of the bowl with a rubber spatula. Reduce the speed to low and gradually add the egg white mixture, and beat for 1 more minute. Divide the batter evenly among the cupcake liners.

5 Bake until a wooden pick inserted into the center comes out with a few crumbs, 17 to 19 minutes. Carefully remove the cupcakes from the pan immediately, put them on a wire rack, and let cool completely.

6 Fill a pastry bag fitted with the #887 decorating tip two-thirds full with one of the flavors of marshmallow frosting and another pastry bag fitted with a large round tip two-thirds full with the other flavor. Holding the pastry bag fitted with the #887 tip at a 90-degree angle, pipe a generous swirl of frosting on top of each cupcake. Pipe a generous swirl of the second flavor directly on top of the existing piped frosting. Top each cupcake with cotton candy and sprinkle with edible stars.

7 The cupcakes will keep loosely covered at room temperature for up to 2 days.

CHALK-A-LOT COOKIES WITH EDIBLE CHALK

Kids will not only love that they can chalk-scribble all over these chocolate sugar cookies disguised as little chalkboards, but they'll think it's pretty cool that they gobble up the cookie *and* the chalk when they're done. Now that's a wee-one's idea of craft-time cleanup! I like to use a bigger cookie to provide more room for coloring, but any size will do. While kids love making and eating these cookies themselves, I bet they'd relish giving them away as teachers' gifts or to fellow classmates. (If you're feeling the chalkboard love, you might also like the Chalk-a-Lot Cake, page 111.)

1 recipe Dark Chocolate Sugar Cutout Cookies dough (page 167), chilled

Confectioners' sugar, for rolling and dusting fondant

1 pound plus 8 ounces (750 g) black ready-to-use fondant (I use Satin Ice brand for a chalkboard finish)

Piping jelly or fruit jelly

Edible Chalk (recipe follows)

TOOLS

5-inch-wide plaque-shaped cookie cutter

Small rolling pin with ⅛-inch guides

Small offset palette knife

Artist's palette knife

1 Roll out the cookie dough and chill according to the recipe on page 167.

2 Preheat the oven to 350°F (180°C). Cut out the cookies using a large plaque cutter. Chill and bake according to the recipe on page 167, and let cool completely.

3 Dust a work surface with confectioners' sugar and roll out a lemon-size ball of black fondant to ⅛-inch thickness. Cut out fondant plaques with the same cutter you used for the cookies. Let the fondant sit to firm up, about 30 minutes.

4 Using a small offset palette knife, spread a small amount of jelly onto the cookies, and using an artist's palette knife, gently transfer each of the fondant pieces to the cookies. Gently press into place using your fingers to smooth the edges and let the fondant dry completely, at least 2 hours.

5 Serve the cookies with edible chalk, and let them doodle till they drop!

RECIPE CONTINUES

6 ounces (170 g) candy coating in desired color (I like Wilton)

1 (4 g) jar petal dust or luster in coordinating color

Confectioners' sugar, for dusting

TOOLS

5 plastic 8 × ½-inch cake dowel straws (or jumbo drinking straws, as long as they are sturdy)

One ¼-inch wooden dowel 12 inches long

NOTE: If you find the chalk really doesn't want to come out of the straw, use a craft blade (I use X-Acto) to carefully cut the straw down the middle, then remove.

EDIBLE CHALK
MAKES ABOUT FIFTEEN 2-INCH PIECES OF CHALK

Use this colorful candy chalk with these cookies or with Chalk-a-Lot Cake (page 111). Or, of course, you can always just snack on them, as you wish. You can play with the colors to easily create many more pieces in an array of hues.

1 Melt the candy coating in a microwave-safe bowl in 20-second intervals, stirring with a spatula after each one. Add the petal dust and stir until completely incorporated. (For a more intense color, add more dust.) Pour the candy into a plastic zip-top bag and snip a small hole in one corner. Fill each straw with the candy. Put the straws in the freezer until the candy is set, about 5 minutes.

2 Remove the filled straws from the freezer, and using the wooden dowel, push the hardened candy out of the straw. The "chalk" should slide right out. If still too soft, put it back in the freezer for another 3 minutes. Cut each chalk into three even pieces. Dust with confectioners' sugar for a chalky effect, if desired.

3 The chalk will keep in a plastic zip-top bag in a cool, dry place away from direct sunlight for up to 8 weeks.

CUT & PASTE ILLUSTRATION CAKE

MAKES ABOUT 15 SERVINGS

Okay, now it's time to watch the little ones make the magic. Let kids become the main cake designers, creating their own hand-illustrated cake with all drawings cut and pasted by them. I find that a three-tiered cake makes the artists feel particularly legit, but you can customize shape, color, scale, and more—the sky is the limit. Just hand them the edible food markers and edible decorating paper, and they will do the rest. Any variety of cake layers works great, but I find when it comes to kids, confetti cake often solicits smiles aplenty.

1 recipe Pastel Vanilla Birthday Cake batter (page 78)

2 recipes Swiss Meringue Buttercream (page 176), flavored as desired

3 pounds (1½ kg) white ready-to-use fondant

AmeriColor gel paste food color in Electric Blue

Shortening or piping jelly

TOOLS

4-inch, 5-inch, and 6-inch thin round cake boards

Edible food markers (I like Kopycake or AmeriColor)

2 to 4 sheets edible decorating paper (I like Wilton Sugar Sheets)

Dowels

8- or 9-inch cake drum or platter

Food-safe paintbrushes

1 Preheat the oven to 350°F (180°C). Grease the bottoms of three 4 × 2-inch, three 5 × 2-inch, and three 6 × 2-inch round cake pans and line with parchment.

2 Divide the cake batter among the cake pans. Bake in the center of the oven until a wooden pick inserted in the center comes out with a few crumbs, 20 to 25 minutes. Repeat with the final layers. Let the cakes cool in the pans on wire racks for 10 minutes. Run a knife around the edges to loosen, and carefully turn the layers out onto wire racks. Peel off the paper, and let cool completely.

3 Fill and frost all three tiers of cake and prepare them for covering with fondant (see page 135 for instructions). Refrigerate until very firm, at least 1 hour.

4 Tint the fondant a very bright blue using 25 to 30 drops (½ teaspoon) of the gel paste food color (you will want to start with about 15, knead to blend, and then add the color in 5-drop increments until you have reached the desired shade). Once you are pleased with the color, divide the fondant by weighing out three separate quantities and sealing each in a plastic zip-top bag: 1 pound plus 2 ounces (510 g) for the 6-inch tier, 1 pound (454 g) for the 5-inch tier, and 12 ounces (340 g) for the 4-inch tier.

5 Cover each of the three tiers with fondant (see page 139 for instructions). Refrigerate the cakes for at least 1 hour.

RECIPE CONTINUES

Let your cakelets
get creative with
the cutout shapes.

cakelets
IN THE KITCHEN

If kids are stumped on what to draw, give them inspiration by offering up some of their storybooks or other illustrated tidbits for ideas (this always works for my kids).

6 Meanwhile, give the artists the edible food markers and edible paper and let them draw their hearts out, guiding them to keep the scale and size of the tiers in mind. Have them cut out their drawn shapes, or if they are too young for cutting, you can cut out their shapes for them. Keep the cutouts sealed in a plastic zip-top bag until you are ready to attach them to the cake, as they will lose their pliability when exposed to air.

7 Dowel and stack the cake tiers on your cake drum or platter (see page 142 for instructions). Help the children stick the cutouts to the cake using a thin layer of shortening or piping jelly and a paintbrush.

8 The cake will keep at cool room temperature for up to 24 hours, and then refrigerated for up to 3 days.

NOTES: You can use regular wafer paper or rice paper, but it's more transparent, so double up each of the cutouts to create a more opaque look. ◄ A rainbow cake under all of that sky-blue fondant would kick this cake up another notch and would be such a festive addition to this cake design.

WOW FACTOR WITH NOW FACTOR

If there's no time to work with the fondant, skip it and simply tint the buttercream a bright blue (just know that the buttercream will lend a warm ivory tinge to the color) and stick the cutouts directly on the buttercream.

RAINBOW DOODLE COOKIES

MAKES ABOUT 24 COOKIES

Nothing says "kids" like rainbows, cookies, and colorful markers. Because the cookies are iced completely white to create a blank canvas, this is a great chance to get creative with the shapes and to let the kids choose their favorites—I've never seen my kids as happy as when I hand them my unthinkably huge collection of cookie cutters to rummage through. It keeps them busy, makes them excited, and keeps them involved. And they still get to decorate the cookies! You can also make these with the confetti variation of the cookies just to throw in another hit of rainbow, but you can choose any cutout cookies you wish.

1 recipe Vanilla Sugar Cutout Cookies dough (page 163), chilled

2 recipes Royal Icing (page 194), flavored as desired

TOOLS

Cookie cutters in desired shapes

Pastry bag

Coupler

Decorating tip #3

Edible food markers (I like Kopycake or AmeriColor)

1 Roll out the cookie dough and chill according to the recipe on page 163.

2 Preheat the oven to 350°F (180°C). Cut out the cookies out using the desired cookie cutters. Chill and bake according to the recipe (see page 163) and let cool completely.

3 Outline and fill each cookie shape with the royal icing (see page 133 for instructions). Let sit until completely dry, at least 12 hours.

4 Once the cookies are completely dry and firm, let the kids draw whatever they wish using the edible markers. Let the ink dry for at least 1 hour before touching.

5 The cookies will keep in an airtight container for up to 1 week.

NOTE: Another artsy option for these cookies is for kids to paint the cookies with edible paint, as they do with the Painted Mini Cakes (page 39). Let the paint dry before stacking or packaging the cookies.

SUGAR-COATED
CUTOUT COOKIES

JUMBO FROSTED
ANIMAL CRACKERS

· · · · · · · · · · · · · · · ·

PASTEL-FRAMED
CHALKBOARD COOKIES

· · · · · · · · · · · · · · · ·

WATERCOLOR GRAFFITI
COOKIES

· · · · · · · · · · · · · · · ·

MENAGERIE MASQUERADE
COOKIES

· · · · · · · · · · · · · · · ·

PASTEL PAINTS
COOKIES

· · · · · · · · · · · · · · · ·

ICE CREAM CONE
COOKIE POPS

· · · · · · · · · · · · · · · ·

PINK COTTON CANDY
CLOUD COOKIES

· · · · · · · · · · · · · · · ·

JUMBO FROSTED ANIMAL CRACKERS

MAKES ABOUT 10 LARGE COOKIES

Of all the store-bought animal crackers out there, to me the ultimate variation is those that are a mix of buttery vanilla-lemon cookie and crisp and crunchy cracker. While there are many recipes for these treats, I was determined to mimic the nostalgic flavor of those packaged ones and keep them super-airy, buttery, and crunchy. To really tickle our childhood fancy, I make them jumbo size, coat them in a bright pink glaze, and top them with colorful sprinkles.

2¼ cups (300 g) all-purpose flour

1 cup (110 g) oat flour or whole wheat flour, sifted

½ teaspoon salt

1 cup (225 g) unsalted butter, room temperature

1 cup (205 g) superfine sugar

2 teaspoons pure vanilla extract or Princess Bakery Emulsion (see Note, page 148)

½ teaspoon baker's ammonia (see Note)

¼ teaspoon lemon extract

1 large egg

2 recipes Confectioners' Glaze (page 201) in pink

Rainbow nonpareils

TOOLS

Two ¼-inch wooden dowels

Large animal cookie cutters

1 In a large bowl, whisk together the flours and salt.

2 In the bowl of an electric mixer fitted with the paddle attachment, beat the butter and sugar on medium speed until it becomes a pale paste (you don't want it to be super-fluffy), 2 minutes. In a small bowl, combine the vanilla and baker's ammonia, and then add the mixture to the butter, followed by the lemon extract and the egg. Beat until well incorporated, about 1 minute, scraping the sides of the bowl with a rubber spatula. Reduce the mixer speed to the lowest setting and gradually add the flour mixture, beating until all of the dry ingredients are just incorporated. Do not over-mix. Wrap the dough in plastic wrap, and press it into a large disc. Refrigerate for 1 hour.

3 Unwrap the chilled dough and put it on a large piece of parchment paper. Put a wooden dowel on each side of the dough and put another sheet of parchment paper on top. Roll out the dough until it's level with the dowels. Slide the parchment paper and dough onto a board and refrigerate for 30 minutes or freeze for 15 minutes.

4 Preheat the oven to 350°F (180°C). Line two baking sheets with silicone baking mats or parchment.

5 Remove the dough from the fridge, cut out shapes using the cutters of your choice, and put them on the prepared baking sheets, about 1½ inches apart. Freeze for another 15 minutes.

6 Bake until the cookies are starting to turn a light golden color, about 18 minutes. The cookies will puff up in the oven, but will fall back while cooling. Put the baking sheets on wire racks and let cool for 10 minutes. Gently transfer the cookies to the wire racks and let cool completely. (The cookies will keep in an airtight container at room temperature for 1 week, or in the freezer for up to 2 months.)

7 Put a wire cooling rack over a baking sheet. Using a spoon, pour the confectioners' glaze over each cookie, letting the excess drip onto the baking sheet. Sprinkle with rainbow nonpareils and let dry completely, about 1 hour.

8 The decorated cookies will keep in an airtight container at room temperature for up to 1 week.

NOTE: Baker's ammonia is also known as ammonium carbonate, and it is an old-fashioned leavening ingredient (it's also referred to as hartshorn salts). It's ideal for creating cookies or crackers that are really crispy without an alkaline flavor, which is why I love using it for these animal crackers. You will notice that it has a very strong (and not so pleasant) smell that will waft through your kitchen while the cookies bake, but after baking, it will completely dissipate. If you can't get baker's ammonia for this recipe, you can substitute ½ teaspoon baking powder and ½ teaspoon baking soda, added along with the dry ingredients.

PASTEL-FRAMED CHALKBOARD COOKIES

MAKES ABOUT 20 COOKIES

Ever since my girls and I found some oversize revamped pastel-framed chalkboards at a local vintage shop, I've wanted to turn them into cookies. I find there's something mysterious about the blank chalkboard and ornate frame atop the Black Velvet cookies. These would make unique and tasty place cards for a dinner party, tea party, or wedding—simply use a fine, food-safe paintbrush dipped in white gel paste food color to write the guest's name on each cookie, let dry, wrap in a crystal cellophane bag, tie with ribbon, and set at each place.

1 recipe Black Velvet Sugar Cutout Cookies dough (page 168), chilled

9 ounces (250 g) white ready-to-use fondant

9 ounces (250 g) Candy Clay (page 198) in white

AmeriColor gel paste food colors in Deep Pink, Regal Purple, and Turquoise

Confectioners' sugar, for rolling and dusting fondant

1 pound, 5 ounces (600 g) black ready-to-use fondant (I use Satin Ice for a chalkboard finish)

Piping jelly or fruit jelly

TOOLS

3½-inch-long oval cookie cutter

Small rolling pin with ⅛-inch guides

Small offset palette knife

Artist's palette knife

3½-inch-long silicone plaque mold

1 Roll out the cookie dough and chill according to the recipe on page 168.

2 Preheat the oven to 350°F (180°C). Cut out the cookies using the oval cookie cutter. Chill and bake according to the recipe on page 168, and let cool completely.

3 Knead the white fondant and white candy clay together until well combined, and divide into three portions. Tint one third pale pink using a drop or two of Deep Pink gel paste; tint a second third pale purple using a drop or two of Regal Purple gel paste; tint the final third pale turquoise using Turquoise gel paste. Wrap each separately in a small plastic zip-top bag. Set aside.

4 Dust a work surface with confectioners' sugar and roll out a plum-size ball of black fondant to ⅛-inch thickness. Cut out as many ovals as you have cookies, using the same cookie cutter. Let the fondant ovals sit until they firm up, about 30 minutes.

5 Using a small offset palette knife, spread a small amount of jelly onto each cookie. Using an artist's palette knife, gently transfer each of the fondant pieces to the cookies and gently press into place.

6 Dust the plaque mold with confectioners' sugar and fill it with one of the colors of the candy clay mixture, trimming off any excess with the artist's palette knife. Freeze for about 1 minute, and then carefully remove the frame from the mold. Using a toothpick, apply a few small dabs of piping jelly to the underside of the frame and gently press it into place on the cookie.

7 The cookies will keep in a box with some airflow for up to 1 week.

WATERCOLOR GRAFFITI COOKIES

MAKES ABOUT 20 COOKIES

These colorful cookies came to me after I fell in love with painting the Watercolor Graffiti Cake (page 115). I experimented with a few (new for me) classic watercolor painting techniques to create these fun treats. Since I'm not a fine artist, I can assure you that you certainly don't need to be one, either—this technique is so easy and the results can be stunning. If you like the lacquered effect, simply paint on some edible varnish. I opted for a cotton candy color palette, but of course you can use any colors you love. Add sugar flowers or candy beads if you like, or leave the cookies as they are—pure cookie art.

1 recipe Vanilla Sugar Cutout Cookies dough (page 163), flavored as desired and chilled

7 ounces (200 g) white ready-to-use fondant

7 ounces (200 g) Candy Clay (page 198) in white

Confectioners' sugar, for rolling and dusting

Piping jelly or fruit jelly

AmeriColor gel paste food colors in Regal Purple, Deep Pink, and Sky Blue

Vodka

Disco dust in light blue and purple (I like CK Products)

24-karat gold luster dust

24-karat gold flakes (optional)

TOOLS

Round 3½-inch cookie cutter

Small rolling pin with ⅛-inch guides

Small offset palette knife

Artist's palette knife

Five 1-inch round sponge applicators (I like Plaid brand Spouncers)

Food-safe paintbrush

1 Roll out the cookie dough and chill according to the recipe on page 163.

2 Preheat the oven to 350°F (180°C). Cut out the cookies using the round cookie cutter. Chill and bake according to the recipe on page 163, and let cool completely.

3 Knead the white fondant and white candy clay together until well combined, and seal in a plastic zip-top bag. Dust a work surface with confectioners' sugar. Pinch a plum-size ball off the candy clay mixture and roll it out to ⅛-inch thickness. Cut out as many rounds as you have cookies, using the same cookie cutter. Let the fondant rounds sit to firm up, about 30 minutes.

4 Using a small offset palette knife, spread a small amount of piping jelly onto the cookies. Using an artist's palette knife, gently transfer each of the fondant pieces to the cookies, gently press into place, and use your finger to smooth the edges slightly.

5 Dilute one or two drops of each of the three gel paste colors with a splash of vodka—the more vodka you add, the more washed-out the color will be. Using the sponges, dab the color onto the cookies, letting them merge and blend. Add some clear vodka to soften the colors even further, if desired. Be careful to not over-saturate the surface, or it will break down and become sticky. Press a tissue on what you've painted, and then pull it off to reveal a textured finish. Sprinkle the cookies with a dash of the light blue and purple disco dust for sparkle. Using a fine food-safe paintbrush, mix a small amount of gold luster dust with a drop or two of vodka and paint the edges of the fondant. Spatter a few drops of the gold paint onto the cookies and top with a few gold flakes (if using). Let dry overnight.

6 The cookies will keep in a box or container with some airflow for up to 1 week.

Real gold
flakes!

MENAGERIE MASQUERADE COOKIES

MAKES ABOUT 6 LARGE COOKIES (2 EACH CAT, FOX, AND PANDA COOKIES)

The inspiration for these fancy cookies comes from a collection of sparkly costume masks my girls received as gifts. While they take quite a lot of time to make, they are a spectacular addition to any party. I created a black-as-night Black Velvet Sugar Cutout Cookie recipe (page 168) while designing these cookies because I felt that a regular old cookie just wouldn't do. The black cookies give the masks an enchanting flair and lend a unique velvet flavor (think red velvet cake). For best results, give yourself a couple of days to work slowly and ensure that each color dries properly before adding the next. To make it a little more time-effective, you can bake the cookies as far as one month ahead of time and freeze them. Simply bring the cookies to room temperature when you're ready to use them.

1 recipe Black Velvet Sugar Cutout Cookies dough (page 168), chilled

2 recipes Royal Icing (page 194)

AmeriColor gel paste food colors in Super Black, Violet, Electric Orange, Warm Brown, and Soft Pink

1 cup sanding sugar in orange

1 cup sanding sugar in white

1 cup sanding sugar in black

Disco dust in white, Golden Orange, and black

Instant Edible Varnish (page 200)

TOOLS

Animal face templates (page 205)

8-inch cookie sticks (I like Wilson brand)

3 pastry bags

3 couplers

3 decorating tips #3

Food-safe paintbrushes

Fine-tip black food marker

Black paper straws (optional)

1 Line two baking sheets with silicone baking mats or parchment. Roll out and chill the cookie dough according to the recipe on page 168. Cut out the animal masks using the templates on page 205. Carefully insert one 8-inch cookie stick into the left side of each cookie by gently screwing in the top of the stick about 1½ inches. Gently transfer the cookies to the prepared baking sheets. Freeze the cookies until firm, at least 15 minutes. Meanwhile, preheat the oven to 350°F (180°C).

2 Bake the cookies according to the recipe on page 168 and let cool completely.

3 Tint the icing in separate small bowls as follows: 1 cup icing tinted black using equal parts Super Black and Violet; ¾ cup icing tinted rusty orange using about 4 drops Electric Orange and a drop Warm Brown; ½ cup icing tinted peach using a tiny dab of Electric Orange and Warm Brown (less is more, as it will darken a bit after drying); ¼ cup icing tinted pink using a drop or two of Soft Pink. Leave the remaining icing white. Once each one has been tinted, stir in a few drops of water at a time, until a line in the icing made with a toothpick disappears in 10 seconds (see page 194 for instructions). Keep each bowl of icing covered when not in use.

4 In a small bowl, combine 1 cup orange sanding sugar and 1 drop of Warm Brown gel paste.

RECIPE CONTINUES

NOTE: Before outlining the ears, the pandas' oval eyes, and the foxes' snouts, cut out those areas on the templates and gently hold in place while marking the shapes with a pin. Remove the template pieces and follow the markings when piping.

5 Fit the three pastry bags with couplers and #3 round decorating tips, and fill one with peach icing, one with pink icing, and one with half of the black icing (see page 131 for instructions). Cover the remaining icing and refrigerate until needed (the next day). Keep the tip of each bag tucked into a damp cloth when not in use.

6 **Day 1:** Using the **black** icing: Outline and fill the following areas (see page 133 for instructions): For the *panda*, outline the eyes, ears, and ovals around the eyes. Let dry for about 1 minute and then fill. On a piece of wax paper, pipe two small triangular black panda noses. Set everything aside to dry overnight, or ideally 24 hours. For the *fox*, outline and fill the ears. On a piece of wax paper, pipe two small triangular black fox noses.

Using the **peach** icing: For the *fox*, outline the lower portion of the faces, using the template on page 205. Fill and set aside to dry overnight, or ideally 24 hours.

Using the **pink** icing: For the *cat*, outline and fill the ears, using the template on page 205. Set aside to dry overnight, or ideally 24 hours. Wash and dry all the pastry bags and tips.

7 **Day 2:** Once all of the cookies are dry, remove the bowls of the remaining icing from the fridge and stir until smooth. Fill a pastry bag fitted with a coupler and #3 icing tip with the remaining black icing, another with the orange icing, and a third about one-third full with white icing.

For the *panda*, outline the remaining area with white icing and fill. Sprinkle with white sanding sugar and white disco dust. Let dry completely, ideally overnight.

For the *fox*, outline the remaining area with orange and fill. Sprinkle with the orange sanding sugar and orange disco dust. Let dry completely, ideally overnight.

For the *cat*, outline the eyes and then the perimeter of the face with black icing. Fill, and then sprinkle with black sanding sugar and black disco dust. Let dry completely, ideally overnight.

8 Using a dry food-safe paintbrush, brush any excess glitter from the dried cookies, and using a pin, pick off any stray sanding sugar extending over the smooth areas. Using a clean food-safe paintbrush, paint the edible varnish on all of the ears and the panda's eyes. Using a fine-tip black food marker and a small ruler, draw on the foxes' whiskers. Adhere a black nose onto each fox and a pink nose onto each cat with a dab of royal icing. Paint the noses with the edible varnish. Let dry completely.

9 The cookies will keep in an airtight container at room temperature for up to 2 weeks.

PASTEL PAINTS COOKIES

MAKES ABOUT 10 LARGE COOKIES

I don't know what it is with my love of painting-inspired cookies, but I think they bring a whimsy and wonder to classic sugar cookies that speak to the artist in all of us. Perhaps it's memories of kindergarten painting, which was always the highlight of my days at school. I find with this style of well-loved, well-used pastel paint palettes there's a more authentic and charming look, leaving you to wonder what the artist created before he or she left these palettes behind. Needless to say, no two cookies are the same, but they are all seriously scrumptious. (See photograph, page 60.)

1 recipe Vanilla Sugar Cutout Cookies dough (page 163), flavored as desired, chilled

7 ounces (200 g) white ready-to-use fondant

7 ounces (200 g) Candy Clay (page 198) in white

Confectioners' sugar, for rolling and dusting

2 recipes Royal Icing (page 194)

AmeriColor gel paste colors in Violet, Soft Pink, Sky Blue, Turquoise, Orange, and Bright White

TOOLS

Large quilting ruler

Small rolling pin with ⅛-inch guides

Two small round cookie cutters, about ⅛-inch difference in size

Pastry bags

Artist's plastic palette

Food-safe paintbrushes

Artist's palette knife

1 Line two baking sheets with silicone baking mats or parchment. Roll out the cookie dough and chill according to the recipe on page 163. Cut cookies into 6 × 3¼-inch rectangles, place on the prepared baking sheets, and chill according to the recipe on page 163.

2 Preheat the oven to 350°F (180°C). Bake the cookies according to the recipe on page 163, and let cool completely.

3 Knead the white fondant and white candy clay together until well combined. Dust a work surface with confectioners' sugar and roll out the mixture to ⅛-inch thickness. Cut out 80 circles using your larger round cutter and let sit until slightly firm, about 15 minutes. Using an artist's palette knife, flip the circles upside down and let them sit for a few minutes. Press smaller circles inside the existing circles using the slightly smaller round cutter, creating a border around the edge. Let sit overnight to dry.

4 Outline and fill the cookies with white royal icing (see page 133 for instructions). Let dry completely, ideally overnight.

5 Using royal icing, "glue" 8 circles (or "paint pads") onto each cookie, lined up with 4 on each side.

6 Mix your colors in an artist's palette, using bright white as the base for each one (this gives it that chalky paint look, rather than a watercolor effect). Paint onto the circles and surface of the cookies for a realistic look.

7 The cookies will keep in an airtight container for up to 2 weeks.

ICE CREAM CONE COOKIE POPS

MAKES ABOUT 12 MEDIUM COOKIES

I have something to confess: I'm not an ice cream fanatic. I know it's almost unthinkable, and it's certainly unexpected, but ice cream is just not what sets my heart aflutter (that doesn't include the Campfire variety that inspired the Campfire Deluxe Cake, page 87—that's in a class of its own). But ice cream cone cookies? That's an entirely different story. I've perched these cookies on sticks because there's something about the quirky cones all askew that I find charming. And the contrast of pastel icing with the dark chocolate and sprinkles has a sweet nostalgia that shouts "summer stroll on the boardwalk."

1 recipe Dark Chocolate Sugar Cutout Cookies dough (page 167), chilled

2 recipes Royal Icing (page 194)

AmeriColor gel paste food colors in Chocolate Brown, Super Black, Soft Pink, and Turquoise

Rainbow nonpareils

Gumballs

TOOLS

Ice cream cone cookie cutter

8-inch cookie sticks (I like Wilton brand)

4 pastry bags

4 couplers

3 decorating tips #3

1 decorating tip #2

Paper straws (optional)

1 Line two baking sheets with silicone baking mats or parchment.

2 Roll out and chill the cookie dough according to the recipe on page 167. Cut out the cookies using an ice cream cone cookie cutter. Carefully insert one 8-inch cookie stick by gently screwing in the top of the stick about 1½ inches. Gently transfer the cookies to the prepared baking sheets (6 to a sheet). Freeze the cookies on the baking sheets until firm, at least 15 minutes.

3 Preheat the oven to 350°F (180°C). Bake the cookies according to the recipe on page 167, and let cool completely.

4 Tint about 1½ cups of the icing chocolate brown, using a few drops of Chocolate Brown and Super Black. Put about ¾ cup of chocolate brown icing in a small bowl and cover with plastic wrap. To the remaining ¾ cup chocolate brown icing add just enough water to achieve the 10-second consistency icing (see page 194 for instructions). Tint about ¾ cup of icing pastel pink, using a drop of Soft Pink; and tint another ¾ cup of icing pastel turquoise, using a drop of Turquoise. Stir a few drops of water into each pastel icing to achieve the 10-second consistency icing. Cover the bowls with plastic wrap and keep them covered when not using.

5 Fit three pastry bags with the couplers and #3 decorating tips, and fill each bag with one of the 10-second consistency icings (see page 131 for instructions). Fit another pastry bag with a coupler and #2 decorating tip and fill it with the thicker chocolate brown icing. Keep the tip of each bag tucked into a damp cloth when not in use.

6 Starting with the 10-second brown icing, outline and fill the ice cream cone parts of the cookies (see page 133 for instructions). While the cones are drying, use the pastel pink icing to outline and fill the top scoop of each ice cream. Sprinkle the pink icing with rainbow nonpareils. Let dry for at least 30 minutes.

7 Use the thicker brown icing to pipe diagonal lines across the cones.

8 Add a dollop of icing to the very top of the cookies, and attach a gumball "cherry." Outline and fill the bottom scoops of ice cream with the turquoise icing. Let dry overnight, or 24 hours.

9 Slide a paper straw over each cookie stick, if desired.

10 The dry cookies will keep in cellophane bags or layered between wax paper in an airtight container for up to 2 weeks.

PINK COTTON CANDY CLOUD COOKIES

MAKES ABOUT 18 COOKIES

Don't you find that sometimes just the shape of a cookie can make it more delicious? Okay, true, there's more going on here than just shape—confetti sugar cookies on sticks and covered in sweet cotton candy frosting and topped with poofs of cotton candy and silver stars. But even so, I'm convinced that the cloud shape lends a heightened experience. As a loyal devotee of the sweets-obsessed fine artist Will Cotton, I am infinitely inspired by his gorgeous work. These cookies are a celebration of Mr. Cotton and his depiction of a pink-cotton-candy-cloud-lounging Katy Perry.

1 recipe Vanilla Sugar Cutout Cookies dough (page 163), confetti variation made with pink sprinkles, chilled

1 recipe Vanilla Bakery Frosting (page 180), cotton candy variation in pink

Pink cotton candy

Edible silver stars

TOOLS

Cloud cookie cutter

8-inch cookie sticks (I like Wilton brand)

Pastry bag

Decorating tip #1A

Small offset spatula

Light blue paper straws (optional)

Ribbon (optional)

1 Line two baking sheets with silicone baking mats or parchment.

2 Roll out the cookie dough and chill according to the recipe on page 163. Cut out the cookies using the cloud cookie cutter. Carefully insert one 8-inch cookie stick into the bottom of each cloud cookie by gently screwing in the top of the stick about 1½ inches. Gently transfer the cookies to the prepared baking sheets. Freeze the cookies until firm, at least 15 minutes. Meanwhile, preheat the oven to 350°F (180°C).

3 Bake the cookies according to the recipe on page 163, and then let them cool completely.

4 Fit a pastry bag with a large round decorating tip and fill it two-thirds full with cotton candy bakery frosting (see page 131 for instructions). Top each cookie with frosting, leaving about ¼ inch around the edges. Using a small offset spatula, swirl the frosting, pushing it to the edge of the cookies.

5 Top each frosted cookie with a poof of pink cotton candy and a sprinkle of edible silver stars. Slide a baby blue paper straw over the cookie stick and tie a small ribbon where the cookie meets the stick, if desired.

6 The frosted cookies will keep in an airtight container at room temperature for up to 3 days, but cookies with cotton candy on them should be served the same day.

NOTE: I bought a small countertop cotton candy maker, and I have used it more than I ever thought I would. It's so quick and easy to make cotton candy on a whim, and the fluffy stuff is a memorable topping for cookies, cupcakes, cake, and more. You can buy a carton of candy floss sugar at most party shops and online. While you can buy packaged cotton candy, I find that the homemade stuff lasts a little longer.

FOR THE LOVE OF
LAYER CAKES

PASTEL VANILLA
BIRTHDAY CAKE

· · · · · · · · · · · · · ·

DOUBLE-CHOCOLATE
BIRTHDAY CAKE

· · · · · · · · · · · · · ·

BLUE MOON
DREAM CAKE

· · · · · · · · · · · · · ·

CAMPFIRE DELUXE
CAKE

· · · · · · · · · · · · · ·

NEAPOLITA CAKE

· · · · · · · · · · · · · ·

CLOUD 9 CAKE

· · · · · · · · · · · · · ·

CHOCOLATE ROOT BEER
FLOAT CAKE

· · · · · · · · · · · · · ·

LOVE & BUTTER CAKE

· · · · · · · · · · · · · ·

MINTIEST MERINGUE
CAKE

· · · · · · · · · · · · · ·

PASTEL VANILLA BIRTHDAY CAKE

MAKES ONE 4-LAYER ROUND CAKE (12 TO 14 SERVINGS)

On my blog, vanilla cake posts seem to stir up serious excitement and conversation. And while the classic vanilla cake layers in this dreamy creation celebrate simplicity and nostalgia, the filling shouts "Party!" We nestle vibrant bits of colorful cupcakes, sugar cookie dough, and rainbow sprinkles inside fluffy vanilla frosting before covering the cake in rainbow-jimmy-laden pastel frosting and pink piped borders for the ultimate childhood throwback. Because this on-the-sweeter-side layer cake tends to be such a crowd-pleaser, I believe it belongs in every baker's bag of tricks. My version is a rather tall cake at about 6 inches, but if you want to simplify it slightly, try making a more classic three-layer version following the instructions for the Super White Cake (page 148).

4¾ cups (550 g) cake flour, sifted

2 tablespoons baking powder

1½ teaspoons salt

3⅓ cups (675 g) superfine sugar

1 cup plus 2 tablespoons (255 g) cold unsalted butter, cut into pieces

2¼ cups (540 ml) milk, room temperature

1 tablespoon Princess Bakery Emulsion (see Note, page 148) or pure vanilla extract

1 teaspoon fresh lemon juice

8 large egg whites, room temperature

1 large egg, room temperature

AmeriColor gel paste food colors in Soft Pink and Turquoise

2 recipes Vanilla Bakery Frosting (page 180)

½ cup (75 g) confetti quins

1¼ cups (190 g) rainbow jimmies

Eggless Sugar Cookie Dough (recipe follows), chilled and cut into pieces

1 Preheat the oven to 350°F (180°C). Grease the bottoms of four 8 × 2-inch round cake pans and line with parchment. Line two oven-safe ramekins with cupcake liners.

2 Into the bowl of an electric mixer fitted with the paddle attachment, sift the flour, baking powder, and salt. Add the sugar. With the mixer running on low speed, add the cold butter one piece at a time. Beat until all of the butter has been incorporated, about 3 minutes. The mixture should have a fine crumbly, cornmeal-like texture.

3 In a large measuring cup with a spout, combine two-thirds of the milk, the emulsion, and lemon juice. In a separate large measuring cup, gently whisk the egg whites, egg, and remaining milk.

4 With the mixer running on low speed, gradually add the emulsion mixture and beat for 5 minutes. Scrape the sides and bottom of the bowl with a rubber spatula. Add the egg mixture in three parts, scraping down the sides of the bowl after each addition. Beat for 1 minute. Fill each of the prepared ramekins two-thirds full with batter, and tint one bright pink using Soft Pink gel paste, and the other bright turquoise using Turquoise gel paste. Divide the remaining batter evenly among the prepared cake pans.

RECIPE CONTINUES

Long serrated knife

Nonslip squares

Cake-decorating turntable (optional)

8-inch round thin cake board (optional)

Pastry brush

Small offset palette knife

Pastry bag

Decorating tip #1M

NOTE: For an extra-celebratory hit of sprinkles, turn this vanilla cake into a confetti cake by folding 1 cup of confetti quins into the prepared batter.

5 Bake two pans in the center of the oven until a wooden pick inserted into the center comes out with a few crumbs, 20 to 22 minutes (bake the batter in the ramekins along with the cake layers for 15 to 18 minutes). Repeat with the final layers. Let the cakes cool in the pans on wire racks for 10 minutes. Run a knife around the edges to loosen, and carefully turn the layers out onto wire racks. Peel off the paper, and let cool completely.

6 Using a serrated knife, trim any golden crust off the top or sides of the cake layers. Put a nonslip square on your turntable (if using), followed by a piece of wax paper and another small nonslip square (smaller than your cake board). Place a cake board or plate on top. Put one of the cake layers, top up, on the cake board and brush away any stray crumbs using a dry pastry brush.

7 Transfer 3 cups of the bakery frosting to a medium bowl. Fold in the confetti quins, ½ cup of the rainbow jimmies, and the cookie dough pieces. Using an offset palette knife, spread about 1 cup of the frosting mixture on top of the first layer. Break about one-third of the pink and turquoise cupcakes into pieces and press into the frosting. Repeat until you come to the final cake layer, which you will place top down. Press the cake down gently with your hand to secure the layers.

8 Frost the entire cake with a thin layer of the untinted frosting (see page 135 for instructions). Refrigerate the cake for 15 minutes. Tint about 1½ cups of the frosting pastel pink using Soft Pink gel paste color. Tint the remaining frosting pastel turquoise using a few drops of Turquoise gel paste color. Fold about ¾ cup rainbow jimmies into the turquoise frosting and frost the entire cake. Fill a pastry bag fitted with decorating tip #1M two-thirds full with the pink frosting (see page 131 for instructions) and pipe a border around the top perimeter of the cake: Hold the pastry bag above the cake at a 45-degree angle to the right, squeeze until you have a shell, drag just to the right, and release (don't lift the bag). Repeat all the way around. Pipe the same border around the bottom of the cake.

9 The cake will keep at cool room temperature for up to 3 days.

1 cup (135 g) all-purpose flour

¼ teaspoon salt

¼ cup (60 g) unsalted butter, room temperature

⅓ cup (70 g) superfine sugar

¾ teaspoon pure vanilla extract or Princess Bakery Emulsion (see Note, page 148)

1 tablespoon milk

EGGLESS SUGAR COOKIE DOUGH
MAKES ABOUT ½ POUND

Coming across chunks of cookie dough in a dessert is always a welcome surprise, but since our intention is to eat it raw, I've modified my favorite Vanilla Sugar Cutout Cookies dough (page 163) into an eggless version for popping into anything from frosting to ice cream. Simply store it in the freezer and cut off pieces as needed. Cookie dough addicts rejoice!

1 In a small bowl, whisk together the flour and salt.

2 In the bowl of an electric mixer fitted with the paddle attachment, beat the butter and sugar on medium speed until it becomes a pale paste, 2 minutes. Add the vanilla and beat well. Add the milk and beat until incorporated, about 30 seconds. Reduce the mixer speed to the lowest setting, and gradually add the flour mixture, beating until just incorporated. Wrap the dough in plastic wrap and refrigerate for at least 1 hour.

3 The dough will keep in a plastic zip-top bag in the refrigerator for up to 1 week, or in the freezer for up to 3 months.

VARIATION
» **Eggless Chocolate Chip Cookie Dough:** Substitute the granulated sugar with packed light brown sugar and fold in ¾ cup (130 g) mini chocolate chips.

DOUBLE-CHOCOLATE BIRTHDAY CAKE

MAKES ONE 4-LAYER ROUND CAKE (10 SERVINGS)

Although I went through most of my life a devoted vanilla-birthday-cake kind of girl, I have to tell you that once I got a taste for the good stuff—Belgian chocolate and the like—I have had a special place in my heart for chocolate cake. I kept this chocolate layer cake pretty classic, but I believe the key is the chocolate itself—this is the time to break out the fancy dark chocolate and dark cocoa powder, as they really make this cake sing. The cake layers are dark and extremely chocolaty, and they stay moist for days even after being refrigerated, making this a perfect choice when you want to prepare the cake ahead of time.

1 recipe Simple & Splendid Chocolate Cake batter (page 152)

1 recipe Italian Meringue Buttercream (page 174), chocolate variation

Confetti quins, for decorating

TOOLS
Nonslip squares

Cake-decorating turntable (optional)

7-inch round thin cake board (optional)

Pastry brush

Pastry bag

Decorating tip #887

Small offset palette knife

1 Preheat the oven to 350°F (180°C). Grease the bottoms of four 7 × 2-inch round cake pans and line with parchment.

2 Divide the cake batter among the prepared cake pans. Bake two pans in the center of the oven until a wooden pick inserted into the center comes out with a few crumbs, 22 to 25 minutes. Repeat with the final layers. Let the cakes cool in the pans on wire racks for 10 minutes. Run a knife around the edges to loosen, and carefully turn the layers out onto wire racks. Peel off the paper, and let cool completely. Wrap the cakes in plastic wrap, and refrigerate for 30 minutes.

3 Put a nonslip square on your turntable (if using), followed by a piece of wax paper and another nonslip square (smaller than your cake board). Put a 7-inch cake board or a cake plate on top. Put one of the cake layers, top up, on top and brush away any stray crumbs using a dry pastry brush.

4 Fit a large pastry bag with decorating tip #887, and fill the bag two-thirds full with the chocolate buttercream (see page 131 for instructions). Working from the center out, pipe in a circular motion until you reach the perimeter of the cake layer. Place the next cake layer on top and repeat this step until you come to the final cake layer, which you will place top down. Using a small offset palette knife, smooth the center of the buttercream on top of the cake, leaving the edges as they are. Sprinkle a handful of confetti quins on top and refrigerate for 30 minutes.

5 The cake will keep at cool room temperature for up to 24 hours, and then refrigerated for up to 3 days.

BLUE MOON DREAM CAKE

MAKES ONE 3-LAYER ROUND CAKE (10 TO 12 SERVINGS)

This cake is what my sweet dreams are made of—literally. This honestly has never happened before (or since), but I woke up one morning with this exact cake—every detail—in my head, as though I had dreamed up a recipe. I suppose it's not that shocking, as it's really a cake compilation of sorts—all of my favorite flavors, textures, and colors that I've used in some way on my cakes in the past. But this dream was so specific, right down to the macaron moon (I owe you one, mysterious nighttime muse). What I find most appealing about this color scheme is that the cake flavors match the colors, which always offers an even more decadent dessert experience.

1 recipe Blueberry Cake batter (page 155)

2 recipes Vanilla Bakery Frosting (page 180), lavender variation, untinted

1 recipe Zingy Citrus Curd (page 197), using lemons

1 recipe Whipped Cream Frosting (page 185), lavender variation

9 lemon-flavored French macarons

AmeriColor gel paste food colors in Royal Blue, Regal Purple, Super Black, and Electric Purple

Edible gold stars

TOOLS

Long serrated knife

Nonslip squares

Cake-decorating turntable (optional)

8-inch round thin cake board (optional)

Pastry brush

Pastry bag

Decorating tip #1A

Small and medium offset palette knives

Medium straight palette knife

1 Preheat the oven to 350°F (180°C). Grease the bottoms of three 8 × 2-inch round cake pans and line with parchment.

2 Divide the cake batter among the cake pans. Bake two pans in the center of the oven until a wooden pick inserted in the center comes out with a few crumbs, 22 to 25 minutes. Repeat with the final layer. Let the cakes cool in the pans on wire racks for 10 minutes. Run a knife around the edges to loosen, and carefully turn the layers out onto wire racks. Peel off the paper, and let cool completely.

3 Using a long serrated knife, trim any golden crust off the top or sides of the cake. Put a nonslip square on a turntable (if using), followed by a piece of wax paper and another nonslip square (smaller than the cake board). Put a cake board or plate on top. Put one of the cake layers, top side up, on top and brush away any stray crumbs using a dry pastry brush.

4 Fit a pastry bag fitted with decorating tip #1A (or other large round tip), and fill it two-thirds full with the bakery frosting (see page 131 for instructions). Pipe along the perimeter of the cake layer to create a dam. Spoon about ½ cup of the lemon curd inside the frosting dam and use an offset palette knife to spread it evenly. Spread about 1 cup of the whipped cream frosting on top, and then nestle 4 of the macarons flat onto the whipped cream.

5 Gently place another cake layer on top, top up, and repeat step 4. Gently place the final cake layer, bottom up, on top. Wrap the cake tightly in plastic wrap. Refrigerate for at least 1 hour.

RECIPE CONTINUES

6 Remove the cake from the refrigerator and unwrap. Put the cake back on the turntable, if using, and use your clean small offset palette knife to spread a very thin layer of the remaining whipped cream frosting all over the cake. Frost the cake with a thin layer of the bakery frosting and refrigerate for 30 minutes.

7 Meanwhile, tint one-fourth of the remaining bakery frosting navy blue using 6 parts Royal Blue, 2 parts Regal Purple, and 1 part Super Black. Tint another fourth of the frosting bright purple using equal parts Electric Purple and Regal Purple. Tint another fourth of the frosting bright blue using Royal Blue. Leave the last quarter untinted.

8 Starting on the top of the cake, use an offset palette knife to spread a generous layer of the navy blue frosting, creating an even top with frosting that extends just over the edge. Working around the bottom third of the cake, use a medium straight palette knife to apply a very generous coat of frosting using swirls of white and bright purple, resulting in a paler shade of lavender around the very bottom of the cake. Apply another very generous coat of the bright purple directly above the light purple and work your way around the middle third of the cake. On the upper third of the cake, apply the bright blue frosting. (You should have a lot of excess frosting on the cake.) Holding a straight palette knife at a 45-degree angle against the side of the cake, rotate the turntable with the other hand. Work the colors around the cake as you like—you want the colors to blend slightly, but if you over-blend, the colors will start to become muddied. Work slowly and carefully until you are happy with the effect. Using an offset palette knife, pull the frosting over the top of the cake to smooth (see page 135 for instructions).

9 Add a dollop of white frosting on the top of the cake and nestle the remaining macaron on top (the "moon") and sprinkle the cake with the gold stars. Refrigerate for at least 1 hour.

10 The cake will keep at cool room temperature for up to 8 hours, and then refrigerated for up to 3 days.

CAMPFIRE DELUXE CAKE

MAKES ONE 6-LAYER ROUND CAKE (12 TO 14 SERVINGS)

Years ago when my husband and I started dating, we went to a charming gourmet ice cream shop in Bloomfield, Ontario, near his small hometown. The shop offers the most incredible array of decadent artisan ice cream flavors, with everything from Apple Pie to Peanut Butter and Honey—and there was Campfire Cream ice cream. One spoonful of this stuff, with countless chunks of charred marshmallow, transported me to a warm summer night's campfire with friends. It later came to me that this would make an incredible layer cake. While I shared an earlier version of this cake on my blog, I'm excited to offer this utterly decadent one bearing a few new elements and textures.

1 recipe Simple & Splendid Chocolate Cake batter (page 152)

1½ cups (215 g) crushed graham crackers

¼ cup (60 g) unsalted butter

2 tablespoons packed light brown sugar

1 recipe Chocolate Ganache (page 190), chilled to spreading consistency, about 30 minutes

2 recipes Toasted Marshmallow Frosting (page 184), made separately (see Note)

1 recipe Chocolate Cloud Frosting (page 179), malted chocolate variation

TOOLS

Long serrated knife

Pastry brush

2 small offset palette knives

Cake-decorating turntable (optional)

Pastry bag

Decorating tip #1A

Small culinary torch

1 Preheat the oven to 350°F (180°C). Grease the bottoms of three 8 × 2-inch round cake pans and line with parchment.

2 Divide the cake batter among the prepared cake pans. Bake two pans in the center of the oven until a wooden pick inserted in the center comes out with a few crumbs, 20 to 25 minutes. Repeat with the final layer. Let the cakes cool in the pans on wire racks for 10 minutes. Run a knife around the edges to loosen, and carefully turn the layers out onto wire racks. Peel off the paper, and let cool completely. Wrap the cakes in plastic wrap, and refrigerate for 30 minutes.

3 Preheat the oven to 350°F (180°C). Line a baking sheet with a silicone baking mat or parchment paper.

4 Put the crushed graham crackers in a medium bowl. In a small heatproof measuring cup with a spout, microwave the butter and brown sugar in 10-second intervals until the butter has melted, and stir well. Pour the mixture over the graham crackers and stir to combine. Spread the mixture onto the prepared baking sheet and bake until bubbling and golden brown, 6 to 7 minutes. Let cool completely on a wire rack. (The sugared graham crackers will keep in an airtight container for 3 days.)

5 Using a long serrated knife, torte each cake once so you have a total of 6 layers (see page 135 for instructions). Brush away any stray crumbs using a dry pastry brush. Put one of the cake layers, cut side up, on a cake board or plate.

RECIPE CONTINUES

6 Check that the ganache is firm (it should glide when you spread it—if it gets too firm, you can warm it slightly). Using a small offset palette knife, spread one-fifth of the ganache on top, ensuring it is even and reaches about ½ inch from the edge. Cover the ganache with one-fifth of the cooled graham cracker mixture, gently pressing it into the ganache. Using a clean small offset palette knife, cover the graham crackers with one-fifth of the first recipe of marshmallow frosting. Gently place another cake layer on top, cut side up. Repeat the layers until you come to the final cake layer, which you will place bottom up. Wrap the cake tightly in plastic wrap. Refrigerate for at least 2 hours.

7 Remove the cake from the refrigerator and unwrap. Put the cake on a turntable (if using) and frost the entire cake with the chocolate frosting (see page 135 for instructions). If you like a textured frosting effect, hold your palette knife sideways still against the cake and use the other hand to rotate the turntable. With every rotation of the turntable, slowly move your way up the cake another inch or so. Smooth any excess frosting over the top of the cake. Refrigerate for at least 2 hours.

8 Fit a pastry bag with the large round tip and fill it two-thirds full with the second recipe of marshmallow frosting (see page 131 for instructions). Holding the pastry bag at a 90-degree angle above the cake, pipe large dollops over the top of the cake by gently applying pressure for a few seconds, releasing, and then lifting the pastry bag. Using a small culinary torch, toast the dollops. Serve.

9 The cake will keep at cool room temperature for up to 3 days.

NOTE: I know it might seem a little daunting to make the marshmallow frosting twice, but I promise it will be worth it. Unfortunately, the frosting won't keep for extended periods of time without getting spongy, so it's best done as two separate steps: the first batch for step 6, and the second for step 8.

NEAPOLITA CAKE

MAKES ONE 6-LAYER
ROUND CAKE
(12 TO 14 SERVINGS)

Inspired by Will Cotton's incredible artwork, this cake is a fancy twist on the old-fashioned chocolate, vanilla, and strawberry Neapolitan ice cream. The towering delight boasts alternating layers of fluffy chocolate, vanilla, and sweet Maraschino cherry cake filled with super-creamy cherry frosting and covered with a glossy fudge frosting. I torte the cakes to create a show-stopping six-layer masterpiece, or as my cakelets call this, a "Neapolitan rainbow." Stark white royal icing swags and rosettes give this cake's finishing touches an unmistakably French patisserie flair.

4½ cups (520 g) cake flour, plus more for cherries

3¼ cups (675 g) superfine sugar

2 tablespoons baking powder

1 teaspoon salt

1 cup plus 2 tablespoons (255 g) cold unsalted butter, cut into pieces

2¼ cups (540 ml) milk

1 tablespoon pure vanilla extract

10 large egg whites, room temperature

¼ cup (30 g) Dutch-process dark cocoa powder

¼ cup (60 ml) boiling water

10 (50 g) Maraschino cherries, chopped and blotted dry

1 tablespoon Maraschino cherry juice

AmeriColor gel paste food color in Soft Pink

1 recipe Vanilla Bakery Frosting (page 180), pink cherry variation

1 recipe Glossy Fudge Frosting (page 187)

1 recipe Royal Icing (page 194)

1 Maraschino cherry with stem

1 Preheat the oven to 350°F (180°C). Grease the bottoms of three 8 × 2-inch round cake pans and line with parchment.

2 In the bowl of an electric mixer fitted with the paddle attachment, combine the flour, sugar, baking powder, and salt. With the mixer running on low speed, add the cold butter one piece at a time. Beat until all of the butter has been incorporated, about 3 minutes. The mixture should have a fine crumbly, cornmeal-like texture.

3 In a medium measuring cup with a spout, combine half of the milk and the vanilla. In a large measuring cup, gently whisk the egg whites and remaining milk.

4 Increase the mixer speed to medium-low and gradually add the vanilla mixture and beat for 5 minutes. Scrape the sides and bottom of the bowl with a rubber spatula. Reduce the speed to low and gradually add the egg white mixture. Beat for 2 minutes. Scrape the sides and bottom of the bowl, and fold the batter once or twice to ensure everything has been incorporated.

5 Divide the batter among three bowls. In a small bowl, combine the cocoa powder and boiling water, stirring until smooth. Add the cocoa mixture to one of the bowls of batter and stir well. Toss the chopped cherries in a little flour. Put the cherries, the cherry juice, and a drop of pink gel paste into another bowl of batter, and stir well. Leave the remaining bowl of batter as is. Pour one bowl of batter into each of the prepared cake pans.

6 Bake two pans in the center of the oven until a wooden pick inserted into the center comes out with a few crumbs, 20 to 25 minutes. Repeat with the final layer. Let the cakes cool in the pans on wire racks for 10 minutes. Run a knife along the sides of the cakes to loosen, and carefully turn the cakes out onto wire racks. Peel off the paper liners and let cool completely. Wrap the layers in plastic wrap and refrigerate for 30 minutes.

RECIPE CONTINUES

THE SHOW MUST GO ON

If you aren't happy with any of your piping (this happens!), simply let the royal icing dry and then pick it off with a toothpick. Chill the cake and try again until you are satisfied.

TOOLS

Long serrated knife

Nonslip squares

Cake-decorating turntable (optional)

Pastry brush

Small offset palette knife

Pastry bag

Coupler

Decorating tip #28

NOTE: This cake is incredibly decadent and quite sweet, but I know sometimes sweeter isn't always better. For a lighter, less-sweet version, substitute Swiss Meringue Buttercream (chocolate variation, page 176) for the Glossy Fudge Frosting. Just note that buttercream will give the cake a lighter chocolate brown finish.

7 Using a long serrated knife, torte each layer once so you have a total of 6 layers (see page 135 for instructions). Put a nonslip square on your turntable (if using), followed by a piece of wax paper and another nonslip square. Put an 8-inch cake board or plate on top and put one of the chocolate cake layers, cut side up, on top. Using a dry pastry brush, brush away any stray crumbs. Using a small offset palette knife, spread one-fifth of the cherry frosting on top, reaching ½ inch from the edge. Gently place one of the cherry cake layers on top, cut side up, and spread another fifth of the cherry frosting on top. Place one of the vanilla layers on top and spread another layer of frosting on top. Repeat until you come to the final vanilla layer, which you will place bottom up. Wrap the cake tightly in plastic wrap. Refrigerate for at least 30 minutes.

8 Remove the cake from the refrigerator and unwrap. Frost the outside of the cake with the fudge frosting (see page 135 for instructions). Refrigerate for 15 minutes.

9 Cut out an 8-inch parchment circle and fold it in half, and then in half twice more so you have 8 even pie shapes when you open it up. Remove the cake from the refrigerator. Gently set the parchment circle on top of the cake and use a toothpick to make a mark at the very highest point on the side of the cake (not on the top) where each fold is. These marks will be your guide for piping the swags. Remove the parchment round. Now use the toothpick to make a mark spaced evenly between the existing marks, but this time you will place them one-third of the way down, so about 2½ inches down from the top (use a small ruler for accuracy). These mark where the bottom swags will go.

10 Fit a pastry bag with a coupler and decorating tip #28 and fill it two-thirds full with white royal icing (see page 131 for instructions). Pipe shell swags around the top of the cake: Hold the pastry bag above the cake at a 45-degree angle at the first toothpick mark and squeeze until you have a shell, drag just to the right, and release (don't lift the bag). Continue with this motion, creating a series of "U" shapes connecting one point to another, rotating the turntable after each one. Repeat until you have gone all the way around the cake. Pipe small swirls of icing on the top of the cake where each of the swags meets and one in the middle of the cake. Top the middle swirl with a Maraschino cherry, and serve.

11 The cake will keep at cool room temperature for up to 3 days.

CLOUD 9 CAKE

MAKES ONE 4-LAYER ROUND CAKE (10 SERVINGS)

What it is about dark chocolate that just begs to be paired with raspberry? I've experimented with this berry in my baking more than any other, and I am always delighted with the results. So while daydreaming about how to celebrate these ingredients in the most decadent way possible, I decided to introduce a few more flavors and textures to the mix, thereby creating a fancy raspberry-based Neapolitan trio of sorts. The nine dreamy layers of cake and fillings shouldn't make you leery—most of the components can be prepared in advance, making assembly approachable and, dare I say, a piece of cake.

1 recipe Sky-High Chocolate-Covered Cupcakes batter (page 25)

1 recipe Confettilicious Cupcakes batter, without sprinkles (page 20)

RASPBERRY PUREE

1½ cups (210 g) fresh or frozen raspberries

2 tablespoons superfine sugar

1 teaspoon fresh lemon juice

CHOCOLATE SHORTBREAD CRUMBLE

1 cup (135 g) all-purpose flour

½ cup (65 g) confectioners' sugar

2 tablespoons Dutch-process dark cocoa powder

¼ teaspoon salt

⅓ cup (75 g) cold unsalted butter, cut into cubes

2 recipes Swiss Meringue Buttercream (page 176)

3 ounces (90 g) best-quality dark chocolate, melted and cooled

AmeriColor gel paste food color in Soft Pink (optional)

½ cup (180 g) raspberry preserves

1 recipe Shiny Chocolate Glaze (page 188)

Whipped cream

1 fresh raspberry

1. Preheat the oven to 350°F (180°C). Grease the bottoms of two 7 × 2-inch round cake pans and line with parchment.

2. Divide the chocolate cake batter between the prepared cake pans. Bake until a wooden pick inserted in the center comes out with a few crumbs, 20 to 22 minutes. Let the cakes cool in the pans on wire racks for 10 minutes. Run a knife around the edges to loosen, and carefully turn the layers out onto wire racks. Peel off the paper, and let cool completely.

3. Clean the cake pans and then grease them again and line with parchment again. Divide the Confettilicious cake batter between the prepared cake pans. Bake until a wooden pick inserted in the center comes out with a few crumbs, 20 to 22 minutes. Let the cakes cool in the pans on wire racks for 10 minutes. Run a knife around the edges to loosen, and carefully turn the layers out onto wire racks. Peel off the paper, and let cool completely.

4. Make the raspberry puree: In a small saucepan set over medium heat, cook the raspberries, sugar, and lemon juice, stirring occasionally and breaking up the raspberries with a wooden spoon, until the raspberries have started to break down. Reduce the heat to low and cook until the raspberries have broken down completely and the mixture has thickened slightly, 15 to 20 minutes. Put a fine-mesh sieve over a small bowl. Strain the mixture, using the wooden spoon to push the pulp through the sieve. Discard the solids and let the puree cool. (The puree will keep in an airtight container in the refrigerator for up to 3 days.)

5. Make the chocolate shortbread crumble: Preheat the oven to 300°F (150°C). Line a baking sheet with a silicone baking mat or parchment and set aside. In a medium bowl, combine the flour, confectioners' sugar, cocoa powder, and salt. Using two knives or a

RECIPE CONTINUES

Nine layers
tucked inside!

TOOLS

Long serrated knife

Nonslip squares

Cake-decorating turntable
(optional)

7-inch thin round cake board

3 small offset palette knives

pastry cutter, cut in the cold butter until the mixture is crumbly and the butter pieces are pea size. Transfer the mixture to the prepared baking sheet and spread it into an even layer. Bake for 10 minutes, and then use a heatproof spatula to gently stir and fold the crumbs. Bake until some of the mixture starts crisp, about 10 minutes more. Transfer to a wire rack and let cool. (The crumbs will keep in a plastic zip-top bag at room temperature for up to 1 week.)

6 Make the chocolate buttercream by transferring 2 cups of the vanilla buttercream to a small bowl and stirring in the melted chocolate. Make the raspberry buttercream by putting the remaining vanilla buttercream in the bowl of an electric mixer fitted with the paddle attachment. Beat the buttercream on low speed for a few seconds, and then add ⅓ cup cooled raspberry puree (save any remaining puree for another use). Beat until incorporated. Add a few drops of Soft Pink gel paste, if desired.

7 Using a serrated knife, trim any golden crust off the top and sides of the vanilla cake layers. Put a nonslip square on a turntable (if using), followed by a large piece of wax paper, another nonslip square, and then your cake board or plate. Put one of the chocolate cake layers, top side up, on the cake board, and using a small offset palette knife, spread 1 cup of the chocolate buttercream on top. Cover the buttercream with one-half of the chocolate shortbread crumble. Put one of the vanilla layers on top, top side up, and using a small offset palette knife, spread all of the raspberry preserves on the layer. Repeat these layers until you come to the final vanilla cake layer, which you will place bottom up. Wrap the cake tightly in plastic wrap. Refrigerate for 30 minutes.

8 Replace the wax paper on the turntable with a fresh piece. Remove the cake from the refrigerator and unwrap. Put the cake on the turntable. Frost the entire cake with the raspberry buttercream (see page 135 for instructions). Refrigerate for 1 hour.

9 Prepare the chocolate glaze, or if you made it ahead of time, warm it just enough so it is pourable but not hot. Remove the cake from the refrigerator and put it back on the turntable. Starting in the center of the cake, pour a generous amount of glaze on top. Promptly spread the glaze using a small offset palette knife while rotating the turntable. Spread until the glaze begins to drizzle over the edge. If you aren't pleased with your "drizzle" job, put the cake back in the refrigerator and let the chocolate set up, about 10 minutes. Remove from the fridge and repeat the drizzling. To serve, put a dollop of whipped cream and a fresh raspberry in the center of the cake.

10 The cake will keep at cool room temperature for up to 24 hours, and then refrigerated for up to 3 days.

CHOCOLATE ROOT BEER FLOAT CAKE

MAKES ONE 3-LAYER ROUND CAKE (12 SERVINGS)

This cake celebrates the ever-delightful root beer float, one of the most nostalgic treats in all of the land. Who could have imagined that two simple flavors—vanilla and root beer—could create such a timeless treat? And lucky for us, they pair perfectly with chocolate and cake. This is one seriously dreamy cake!

1 recipe Chocolate Butter Cake batter (page 154), chocolate root beer variation

1 recipe Simple Syrup (page 200), root beer variation

1 recipe Vanilla Bakery Frosting (page 180), vanilla ice cream variation

1 recipe Chocolate Cloud Frosting (page 179), root beer variation

1 recipe Shiny Chocolate Glaze (page 188), root beer variation

Rainbow sprinkles

Maraschino cherry

TOOLS
8-inch round thin cake board (optional)

Pastry brush

Small offset palette knife

Cake-decorating turntable

Pastry comb

Ice cream scoop

1 Preheat the oven to 350°F (180°C). Grease the bottoms of three 8 × 2-inch round cake pans and line with parchment.

2 Divide the cake batter among the prepared pans. Bake two pans in the center of the oven until a wooden pick inserted in the center comes out with a few crumbs, 20 to 25 minutes. Repeat with the final layer. Let the cakes cool in the pans on wire racks for 10 minutes. Run a knife around the edges to loosen, and carefully turn the layers out onto wire racks. Peel off the paper, and let cool completely.

3 Place one of the cake layers, top up, on a cake board or plate. Using a skewer or toothpick, poke about six holes in the cake, and using a pastry brush, spread a generous dose of the simple syrup over the surface. Using a small offset palette knife, spread 1 cup of the ice cream frosting on top, reaching about ½ inch from the edge. Repeat these steps until you come to the final cake layer, which you will place bottom up. Reserve the remaining ice cream frosting. Wrap the cake tightly in plastic wrap. Chill for 15 minutes.

4 Remove the cake from the refrigerator and unwrap. Place the cake on a turntable, and frost the entire cake with the chocolate cloud frosting. Hold a pastry comb steady at a 45-degree angle against the side of the cake and slowly rotate the turntable until you have gone all the way around. Refrigerate for at least 30 minutes.

5 Make the chocolate glaze and let it cool just enough so it won't melt the frosting but will pour freely. Pour just enough to cover the top of the cake, pushing it over the edge with your small offset palette knife. Refrigerate for about 5 minutes. Pour and spread the glaze over the cake a second time. Reserve the remaining glaze for drizzling. Sprinkle the top of the cake with rainbow sprinkles.

6 Use an ice cream scoop to scoop the remaining ice cream frosting onto the top of the cake. Drizzle with the remaining chocolate glaze, sprinkle with more rainbow sprinkles, and top with a cherry.

7 The cake will keep at cool room temperature for up to 3 days.

LOVE & BUTTER CAKE

MAKES ONE 6-LAYER ROUND CAKE (12 TO 14 SERVINGS)

This towering delight is truly all about just two simple things: love and butter. It takes a lot of love, and, well, it takes a lot of butter. But it's so worth it. While this cake has several components, most of them can be made ahead of time, ensuring that the process is much less daunting. Either way, you might just fall in love.

1 recipe Best-Ever Buttermilk Cake batter (page 151)

1 cup (135 g) all-purpose flour

½ cup (100 g) granulated sugar

Pinch of salt

⅓ cup (75 g) cold unsalted butter, cut into cubes

2 recipes Swiss Meringue Buttercream (page 176), made with vanilla bean

Salted Caramel (page 193)

Caramelized Pear Filling (recipe follows)

Love & Butter Vanilla Bean Toffee (recipe follows)

TOOLS

Long serrated knife

Pastry brush

Nonslip squares

Cake-decorating turntable (optional)

Small offset palette knife

Large pastry bag (optional)

Decorating tip #887 (optional)

1 Preheat the oven to 350°F (180°C). Grease the bottoms of three 8 × 2-inch round cake pans and line with parchment.

2 Divide the cake batter among the cake pans. Bake until a wooden pick inserted in the center comes out with a few crumbs, 20 to 25 minutes. Let the cakes cool in the pans on wire racks for 10 minutes. Run a knife around the edges to loosen, and carefully turn the layers out onto wire racks. Peel off the paper, and let cool completely.

3 Line a baking sheet with a silicone baking mat or parchment and set aside.

4 In a medium bowl, combine the flour, sugar, and salt. Using two knives or a pastry cutter, cut in the cold butter until the mixture is crumbly and the butter pieces are pea size. Transfer to the prepared baking sheet and spread into an even layer.

5 Bake for 10 minutes, and then use a heatproof spatula to gently stir and fold the crumbs. Bake until the some of the crumbs begin to turn golden, about 5 minutes more. Transfer the baking sheet to a wire rack and let cool. (The crumbs will keep in a plastic zip-top bag at room temperature for up to 1 week.)

6 Using a long serrated knife, torte the three cake layers so you have a total of six layers (see page 135 for instructions). Using a dry pastry brush, brush away any stray crumbs. Put a nonslip square on a turntable (if using), followed by a large piece of wax paper, then another nonslip square, and then your cake board or cake plate.

7 Put one of the cake layers, cut side up, onto the cake board, and using a small offset palette knife, spread a thin layer of the buttercream on top. Spread one-half of the caramel on top of the buttercream, and then cover the caramel with one-half of

RECIPE CONTINUES

the shortbread crumble. Put the next cake layer on top, cut side up, spread another thin layer of buttercream on top, and spoon half of the pear filling over the buttercream, gently spreading it over the layer. Put the next cake layer on and spread 1 cup of the buttercream on top, and top with the next cake layer. Repeat these layers until you come to the final cake layer, which you will place bottom up. Wrap the cake tightly in plastic wrap. Refrigerate for 30 minutes.

8 Remove the cake from the refrigerator and unwrap. Put the cake back onto the turntable (if using) and frost the entire outside with the buttercream (see page 135 for instructions). Put about 1 cup of buttercream in a pastry bag for piping a border around the top of the cake (optional). Put the cake on a baking sheet and use the palm of your hand to gently cover the sides of the cake with the toffee pieces. Pipe a border around the top using the decorating tip, if desired.

9 The cake will keep at cool room temperature for up to 24 hours, and then in the refrigerator for up to 2 days.

6 firm D'Anjou or Bosc pears, peeled, cored, and finely chopped

4 teaspoons fresh lemon juice

2 tablespoons unsalted butter

2 tablespoons packed light brown sugar

¼ teaspoon ground cardamom

¼ teaspoon ground cinnamon

Pinch of salt

CARAMELIZED PEAR FILLING
MAKES ABOUT 2 CUPS

Use this delightful filling warm or cold in cakes, on pancakes, in French toast, over ice cream and more, for a comforting punch of pear, sugar, and spice.

1 In a medium bowl, toss the pears with the lemon juice.

2 In a medium skillet set over medium-low heat, melt the butter until bubbly. Add the pears and increase the heat to medium-high. Cook, stirring occasionally, until the pears begin to break down and soften, 3 to 4 minutes.

3 In a small bowl, combine the brown sugar, cardamom, cinnamon, and salt. Add the mixture to the skillet and cook, stirring occasionally, until the mixture has caramelized, the liquid has thickened, and the pears are tender, 4 to 6 minutes. Remove the pan from the heat and let cool. Transfer to a jar. (The pears will keep in the refrigerator for up to 1 week.)

1 cup (225 g) unsalted butter, cut into cubes

¾ cup plus 2 tablespoons (180 g) granulated sugar

¼ cup (55 g) packed light brown sugar

½ teaspoon sea salt

1 teaspoon vanilla bean paste or seeds of ½ vanilla bean or 1½ teaspoons of pure vanilla extract

¼ teaspoon baking soda

TOOLS

Nonstick cooking spray

Candy thermometer

Small offset palette knife

LOVE & BUTTER VANILLA BEAN TOFFEE

MAKES ABOUT 1 POUND

This old-fashioned, super-sweet, crunchy, and most-buttery toffee is among the most decadent confections I've ever made. It feels good to make it, and it feels incredibly good to give it. You don't have to use a vanilla bean (vanilla extract will still do the trick), but I find the bean lends a deeper vanilla flavor and gives the toffee those gorgeous specks of the good stuff.

1   Line a baking sheet with a silicone baking mat or with parchment sprayed with nonstick cooking spray. Set aside.

2   In a medium saucepan set over medium-low heat, melt the butter. Stir in the sugars, salt, and 1 tablespoon water. Cook, stirring, until the sugar has dissolved, about 1 minute. Clip on a candy thermometer, increase the heat to medium-high, and boil, stirring constantly, until the candy thermometer reads 300°F (150°C), about 5 minutes. Promptly remove the saucepan from the heat, and quickly stir in the vanilla bean paste and baking soda. Pour the mixture onto the prepared baking sheet, and using a small offset palette knife, spread the candy into a thin layer. Let it sit at room temperature until completely set, about 30 minutes.

3   Using a large sharp knife, chop the toffee into small bits. (The toffee will keep in an airtight container at room temperature for up to 2 weeks.)

WOW FACTOR WITH NOW FACTOR

To create this cake in less time, you can substitute the Love & Butter Vanilla Bean Toffee with quality store-bought toffee bits, and use quality store-bought salted (or classic) caramel.

MINTIEST MERINGUE CAKE

MAKES ONE 4-LAYER ROUND CAKE (8 TO 10 SERVINGS)

Inspired by my favorite candy cane bark recipe I make with my kids, this meringue cake is a unique twist on a classic layer cake. And while it's a simple flavor pairing of dark chocolate and peppermint, the variety of textures makes this incredibly addictive. Layers of sparkly candy cane–swirled peppermint meringue are filled with dark chocolate ganache, Oreos, candy cane pieces, and peppermint whipped cream frosting, and then the cake is topped with more crushed peppermint—a true holiday delight with a hint of Whoville magic.

8 egg whites, room temperature or warm

½ teaspoon cream of tartar

2 cups (410 g) superfine sugar

½ teaspoon pure peppermint extract

AmeriColor gel paste food color in Super Red

¼ cup (50 g) white sanding sugar

¼ teaspoon white disco dust (optional)

2 recipes Chocolate Ganache (page 190)

14 chocolate sandwich cookies (such as Oreos), broken into quarters

About 1 cup (230 g) crushed classic red and white candy canes, plus more for sprinkling

1 recipe Whipped Cream Frosting (page 185), peppermint variation

1 Position one oven rack in the lower third and one rack in the upper third of your oven. Preheat the oven to 200°F (90°C). Line two baking sheets with parchment. Use a 7-inch cake pan or board as a template and trace two 7-inch circles on each piece of parchment, spacing them evenly. Flip each parchment piece over on the baking sheets.

2 Wipe the stainless steel bowl and whisk of an electric mixer with a lemon juice–dampened paper towel to eliminate any trace of grease. Put the egg whites in the bowl and beat on low speed until foamy, about 30 seconds. Stop the mixer and add the cream of tartar. Turn the speed to medium and beat until soft peaks form, about 1 minute. Increase the speed to medium-high and very gradually add the sugar, one spoonful at a time. Beat on high speed until very stiff peaks form and the meringue is glossy and thick, about 2 minutes. Add the peppermint extract and beat for 1 more minute.

3 Fit a large pastry bag with a large round decorating tip. Dip a small food-safe paintbrush into the red gel paste, and holding the bag in your nondominant hand, paint three evenly spaced lines on the inside of the bag, working from the tip up. Fill the bag two-thirds full with the meringue, and pipe four circles onto the prepared parchment paper, using the lines as your guide. Using a small offset palette knife, gently spread the meringue evenly. Don't overwork. Sprinkle the outer edge of each meringue with sanding sugar and a pinch of disco dust (if using).

4 Bake until the exterior of the meringues is dry and firm, but not brown, rotating the baking sheets every 30 minutes, about 1½ hours total. Turn off the oven and let the meringues dry out further, about 30 more minutes. Transfer the baking sheets to wire racks and let cool completely. Gently peel each meringue off the

parchment paper and set aside. (The meringues will keep in an airtight container, away from humidity, at room temperature for up to 2 weeks.)

5 Refrigerate the ganache until it has firmed to a spreading consistency (it should glide when you spread it), about 30 minutes. Put a nonslip square on a turntable (if using), followed by a piece of wax paper and another small nonslip square (smaller than your cake board). Put a cake board or plate on the turntable, and using a small offset palette knife, spread a dollop of ganache in the center of the plate. Put one meringue on the plate and spread one-third of the ganache on top. Sprinkle the ganache with cookies and candy canes, and using a clean offset palette knife, spread on one-third of the whipped cream frosting. Repeat with the remaining ingredients and place the final meringue layer on top. Sprinkle the top of the cake with more crushed candy canes and serve.

6 The cake will keep at cool room temperature for up to 8 hours, and then refrigerated for up to 3 days.

FANCIFUL
TIERED CAKES

CANDY-COLORED
STRIPED CAKE

· · · · · · · · · · · · · · · ·

CHALK-A-LOT CAKE

· · · · · · · · · · · · · · · ·

SPRINKLE TWINKLE
CAKE

· · · · · · · · · · · · · · · ·

WATERCOLOR GRAFFITI
CAKE

· · · · · · · · · · · · · · · ·

BEADS & BAUBLES CAKE

· · · · · · · · · · · · · · · ·

PASTEL PARTY CAKE

· · · · · · · · · · · · · · · ·

PEPPERMINTY
DREAM CAKE

· · · · · · · · · · · · · · · ·

DOODLES & DAYDREAMS
CAKE

· · · · · · · · · · · · · · · ·

CANDY-COLORED STRIPED CAKE

MAKES ABOUT 24 SERVINGS

What I love about striped cakes is that they can almost look like paper-wrapped confections with a candy-shop-meets-carnival vibe. And while the technique isn't difficult (it's actually rather fun), it's all about the medium: candy clay, or modeling chocolate, which has minimal stretch, a gorgeous sheen, and a sweet taste, making it ideal for this type of work.

Once you get your rhythm down, you'll see that decorating this cake moves quickly. I fell in love with a stripe-making technique originated by talented cake artist Jessica Harris, in which small panels of pattern are created using the candy clay stripes laid upon wax paper and then applied to the cake as a sticker of sorts. Note that the candy clay needs to be made a day ahead.

2 recipes Simple & Splendid Chocolate Cake batter (page 152)

2 recipes Swiss Meringue Buttercream (page 176), flavored as desired

3½ pounds (1¾ kg) white ready-to-use fondant

AmeriColor gel paste food colors in Turquoise and Sky Blue

2 recipes Candy Clay (page 198), white, hot pink, retro orange, and pastel blue variations, made at least 1 day ahead

Candy coating in white

Pink candy beads

Pink circus animal topper (optional; see Note, page 109)

1 Preheat the oven to 350°F (180°C). Grease the bottoms of three 5 × 2-inch, three 6 × 2-inch, and three 7 × 2-inch round cake pans and line with parchment.

2 Divide the cake batter among the prepared cake pans. Bake two pans in the center of the oven until a wooden pick inserted in the center comes out with a few crumbs, 20 to 25 minutes. Repeat with the final layers. Let the cakes cool in the pans on wire racks for 10 minutes. Run a knife around the edges to loosen and carefully turn the layers out onto wire racks. Peel off the paper, and let cool completely.

3 Fill and frost the three tiers of cake with the buttercream on the coordinating round thin cake boards, preparing them for covering with fondant (see page 135 for instructions). Refrigerate until firm, about 1 hour.

4 While the cakes are chilling, tint the fondant to the same pale blue as your candy clay, about 5 drops Turquoise for every drop of Sky Blue. Divide the fondant into three parts as follows, sealing each in a separate plastic zip-top bag: 1 pound plus 6 ounces (630 g) for the 7-inch tier, 1 pound plus 2 ounces (515 g) for the 6-inch tier, and 1 pound (455 g) for the 5-inch tier. Cover each cake in fondant (see page 139 for instructions) and refrigerate until firm, at least 1 hour.

RECIPE CONTINUES

Ready for a
carnival party!

TOOLS

5-inch, 6-inch, and 7-inch round thin cake boards

Fondant mat with measurements

Pasta machine with fettuccini attachment (¼-inch-wide strips) and flat roller

Cake-decorating turntable (optional)

Small ruler

Shortening

Small sharp knife

2-inch round scalloped cookie cutter

Decorating tip #2

¼-inch wooden dowels (I like Wilton)

9- or 10-inch cake drum or platter

5 Meanwhile, prepare the colored strips: Microwave the candy clay for about 10 seconds each to soften. Knead until smooth and workable. On your fondant mat, using a small rolling pin, roll out a plum-size amount of candy clay until it's about ¼ inch thick. Feed it through your pasta machine set to the fettuccini setting, and set aside. Repeat with the remaining candy clay. Loosely cover the strips with plastic wrap until you are ready to decorate.

6 Remove the first tier of fondant-covered cake from the refrigerator, and put it on a turntable, if using. You will create striped panels that are 2 inches wide by about 4 inches tall (measure the height of your cake to determine the exact height). Each will consist of eight ¼-inch-wide strips (four colors side-by-side, repeated once). Cut a small piece of wax paper and tape it on the fondant mat with the straightest edge of the paper at the bottom. Use a paper towel to apply a thin layer of shortening to the wax paper. Lay the colored strips down nice and straight, with no spaces in between. Use a small ruler to straighten the strips after each addition. Using your finger, gently rub along the joins to bind the strips. Use a small sharp knife to trim the top of the panel straight.

7 Apply the striped panel to the cake: Using a paper towel, apply a thin layer of shortening to the cake over an area about the same size as your panel. Gently lift the panel up to the cake, lining up the bottom edge with the bottom edge of your cake, and press the panel against the cake. Gently peel off the wax paper. If your panel isn't straight, use the ruler to gently push it into place.

8 Repeat the panel making and placing steps until you have gone all the way around the cake. Depending on how close together the strips were applied, you might find that you have only enough space for a partial panel when you get to the end. That's okay.

9 Add the scalloped border: Change the pasta machine setting to the flat roller. Roll out a plum-size ball of the blue candy clay and feed it through the pasta roller. Use a 2-inch scalloped circle cookie cutter to cut scalloped circles from the clay. Using the small knife, trim the shapes into half circles about 1 inch tall in the middle. Use the same cutter to gently cut into the stripes on the cake, removing the same size half circle. Use the wax paper to apply the scalloped half circles to the cake as though you were fitting in a puzzle piece. Use your fingers to smooth the scallops into place. Repeat this step until you have gone all the way around.

NOTE: While almost any type of cake topper would look charming on this cake (such as sugar flowers, cake bunting, and more), I felt that the hot-pink elephant just *belongs* perched up there. To create your own pink elephant topper, simply spray-paint a plastic elephant (I found this one in the kids' toy section at a vintage shop) with hot-pink spray paint. Let dry completely before setting on top of the cake.

10 Trim any excess length from the stripes and scallops around the cake tier. Using a small round decorating tip, create a perforated look by impressing tiny circles along the scalloped edges. Use your fingers to smooth any raw edges and to secure the tops of the strips to the cake. Refrigerate the cake.

11 Repeat with the remaining tiers. Keep each tier refrigerated until you are ready to stack the cake.

12 Dowel and stack the cake tiers onto the cake drum (see page 142 for instructions). Put a handful of white candy coating in a small microwave-safe bowl and microwave in 10-second intervals, stirring well, until melted. Transfer to a small plastic zip-top bag, seal, and cut a tiny hole in one of the corners. Use the candy coating to adhere a pink candy bead between each pair of scallops on each tier. Refrigerate the stacked cake for at least 1 hour to let everything firm up.

13 The cake will keep at cool room temperature for up to 24 hours, and then refrigerated for up to 3 days.

LET THEM EAT CAKE!

The numbers of servings noted for each cake in this chapter's recipes are based on what I consider a reasonable party serving size. Party servings are bigger than what you might find in a wedding cake serving guide (wedding cake servings are typically calculated based on 1 × 2 × 4-inch slivers, as it's usually served after dinner and another dessert has been served). I base my cake servings on 2 × 2 × 4-inch-tall servings—that's usually three layers of cake, two layers of buttercream along with any other fillings, and buttercream on the outside and often fondant as well. While that still may sound like a small piece, just remember that things like fondant, ganache, and meringue buttercream are very rich. If you serve larger pieces than this, you might end up with a lot of wasted cake. That being said, for those of us who believe one can never have too big a piece, you will just need to plan accordingly and make a bigger cake.

CHALK-A-LOT CAKE

MAKES ABOUT
28 SERVINGS

Here's a secret—"chalkboard" fondant is just black fondant with a dusting of confectioners' sugar. The key, though, is having chalk that is edible but can still write with a lot of pigment. Of course, you can do this on a one-tier cake for ease, but assembling it in a fancy cake fashion makes it particularly impressive. The white chocolate buttercream filling is tinted a trio of pastel shades to add contrast and visual appeal. The short layer is simply a fondant-covered riser included to add interest because the cake is so much of one solid color.

3 recipes Simple & Splendid Chocolate Cake batter (page 152)

1 recipe Swiss Meringue Buttercream (page 176), white chocolate variation

AmeriColor gel paste food colors in Soft Pink, Regal Purple, and Turquoise

2 recipes Swiss Meringue Buttercream (page 176)

3½ pounds (1¾ kg) black ready-to-use fondant (I prefer Satin Ice brand for this cake)

Edible Chalk (page 54)

Confectioners' sugar, for dusting

TOOLS

5-inch, 6-inch, and 8-inch round thin cake boards

¼-inch wooden dowels

7-inch Styrofoam riser

10-inch round cake drum or platter

Shortening

Large food-safe paintbrush

1 Preheat the oven to 350°F (180°C). Grease the bottoms of three 5 × 2-inch, three 6 × 2-inch, and three 8 × 2-inch round cake pans and line with parchment.

2 Divide the cake batter among the prepared cake pans. Bake two pans in the center of the oven until a wooden pick inserted in the center comes out with a few crumbs, 20 to 25 minutes. Repeat with the final layers. Let the cakes cool in the pans on wire racks for 10 minutes. Run a knife around the edges, and carefully turn the layers out onto wire racks. Peel off the paper, and let cool completely.

3 Divide the white chocolate buttercream into three medium bowls, and tint them, respectively, pastel pink, lavender, and turquoise. Fill the three tiers of cake with the tinted buttercream on the coordinating round thin cake boards. Frost the outside of the cake tiers with the vanilla buttercream, creating a very smooth finish for fondant (see page 135 for instructions).

4 Cover each cake tier in the black fondant (see page 139 for instructions), using 1 pound plus 8 ounces (680 g) for the 8-inch tier, 1 pound (455 g) for the 6-inch tier, and 1 pound (455 g) for the 5-inch tier. Use the remaining fondant to cover the Styrofoam riser as you would a real cake, using a paper towel to apply a thin layer of shortening all over the top and sides of the riser before applying the fondant. Refrigerate the cakes and riser for at least 1 hour.

5 Dowel and stack the tiers (see page 142 for instructions) onto the cake drum or platter. Refrigerate until the fondant is dry, 2 hours.

6 Remove the cake from the fridge and doodle your heart out using the edible chalk. If the fondant becomes sticky from condensation, let it dry before doodling. Using a large dry food-safe paintbrush, dust the cake with a little confectioners' sugar to create a "chalky" finish.

7 The cake will keep at cool room temperature for up to 24 hours, and then refrigerated for up to 3 days.

SPRINKLE TWINKLE CAKE

MAKES ABOUT 18 SERVINGS

Sometimes we just need to get fancy. And nothing says fancy like a teal blue sparkly sequin and glitter–encrusted red velvet cake. This delicious cake is filled and frosted with fluffy cream cheese frosting before being completely covered in a medley of quin sprinkles painted with super-shimmery edible paint. You could use any flavor of cake and frosting, but there's something magical about the contrast of a glittery teal blue frosting and rich red-hued cake.

1 recipe Red Velvet Cake batter (page 157)

1 recipe Swiss Meringue Buttercream (page 176)

Few drops AmeriColor gel paste food color in Teal

1 recipe Fluffy Cream Cheese Frosting (page 183)

About 3 cups (450 g) medley of star and confetti quin sprinkles

1 can lustre spray in blue (I use PME)

1 (4 g) jar luster dust or hybrid sparkle dust in teal (I like Les Chocolats Roxy & Rich sparkle dust in Teal Blue)

Glittered cherries (see page 28 for instructions)

TOOLS

4-inch, 5-inch, and 6-inch round thin cake boards

¼-inch wooden dowels

8-inch cake drum or platter

Nonslip squares

Food-safe paintbrush

1 Preheat the oven to 350°F (180°C). Grease the bottoms of three 4 × 2-inch, three 5 × 2-inch, and three 6 × 2-inch round cake pans and line with parchment.

2 Divide the batter among the prepared cake pans. Bake three pans in the center of the oven until a wooden pick inserted in the center comes out with a few crumbs, 20 to 22 minutes. Repeat with the final layers. Let the cakes cool in the pans on wire racks for 10 minutes. Run a knife around the edges to loosen, and carefully turn the layers out onto wire racks. Peel off the paper, and let cool completely.

3 Tint the Swiss meringue buttercream pastel teal blue using a few drops of Teal gel paste. Fill the cake tiers with the cream cheese frosting on the coordinating round thin cake boards. Frost the cake tiers with the blue buttercream until you achieve a nice, smooth finish (see page 135 for instructions). Refrigerate until firm, about 1 hour.

4 Dowel and stack the cakes onto a cake drum or platter (see page 142 for instructions). Let the cake sit at room temperature until the buttercream is tacky to the touch, about 30 minutes.

5 Carefully place the stacked cake on a baking sheet, and working from the top down, gently press the confetti quin mixture to the frosting using the palms of your hands. Collect the excess quins from the baking sheet and return them to the plastic zip-top bag for another use.

6 Spray the entire cake with the blue lustre spray. While the paint is still wet, sprinkle some of the dry Teal luster dust over the cake.

7 Top with glittered cherries, if desired, and serve.

NOTE: For a quick and easy cake topper, spray-paint a plastic animal or other small toy or smooth-surfaced knickknack with glitter paint. Let dry completely before putting on top of the cake.

8 The cake will keep at cool room temperature for up to 8 hours, and then refrigerated for up to 3 days.

cakelets
IN THE KITCHEN
Try using Styrofoam cake dummies, craft glue, regular craft glitter, decorations, and markers, and let kids design their own wedding cake. You'll be amazed what they come up with!

WATERCOLOR GRAFFITI CAKE

MAKES ABOUT 35 SERVINGS

As I've said before, just because you're not a fine artist doesn't mean you can't make unique and stunning artsy cakes. Watercolor with a textured effect—tossing on random glitter highlights, 24-karat gold splatter, and pretty much anything else your heart desires—creates a stunning effect. I love abstract artistic cakes because when you cut the cake, no two slices are the same. Each one boasts its own colors, bits of gold, and hits of glitter. What I love about this technique is that it's a sit-down-and-listen-to-music and express-yourself cake. There's no wrong pattern, and it's not time-sensitive. You can go back as many times as you wish to blend and add highlights of glitter. Of course, you can do this on any single-tiered cake covered in fondant, but I think the multiple tiers have a spectacular effect.

3 recipes Chocolate Butter Cake batter (page 154)

3 recipes Swiss Meringue Buttercream (page 176), flavored as desired

4¼ pounds (2 kg) white ready-to-use fondant

AmeriColor gel paste food colors in Deep Pink, Sky Blue, and Regal Purple

Vodka or clear lemon extract

Light blue and purple disco dust (I used CK Products Waterfall and Lilac)

24-karat gold highlighter dust

Large white sugar flower (optional)

Bright pink petal dust (optional)

1 ounce (30 g) white candy melts (optional)

1 Preheat the oven to 350°F (180°C). Grease the bottoms of three 5 × 2-inch, three 7 × 2-inch, and three 9 × 2-inch round cake pans and line with parchment.

2 Divide the batter among the prepared cake pans. Bake two pans in the center of the oven until a wooden pick inserted in the center comes out with a few crumbs, 20 to 25 minutes. Repeat with the final layers. Let the cakes cool in the pans on wire racks for 10 minutes. Run a knife around the edges to loosen, and carefully turn the layers out onto wire racks. Peel off the paper, and let cool completely.

3 Fill and frost each cake tier with the buttercream on the coordinating round thin cake boards, preparing them for covering with fondant (see page 135 for instructions). Refrigerate for 1 hour.

4 Cover each tier with the fondant (see page 139 for instructions), using 1 pound plus 14 ounces (850 g) for the 9-inch tier, 1 pound plus 5 ounces (600 g) for the 7-inch tier, and 1 pound plus 1 ounce (485 g) for the 5-inch tier. Refrigerate for 1 more hour. Reserve excess fondant in a plastic zip-top bag.

5 Dowel and stack the chilled tiers (see page 142 for instructions) onto your cake drum. Transfer to the turntable (if using).

6 Squeeze the gel paste colors into small individual bowls and dilute with vodka or lemon extract (about a teaspoon per drop of color). Starting from the top and working down, use the sponges to dab

RECIPE CONTINUES

TOOLS

5-inch, 7-inch, and 9-inch round thin cake boards

¼-inch wooden dowels

12-inch cake drum or platter

Cake-decorating turntable (optional)

Nonslip squares

Small round sponges (I like Plaid brand 1-inch Spouncers)

Food-safe paintbrushes

colors onto the cake. Working on areas that are about 6 inches wide at a time, press a tissue on what you've painted, and then pull it off to reveal a textured finish. Repeat all over the cake, leaving some white space here and there.

7   Blend any harsh lines or areas with a vodka-soaked tissue (the vodka acts as an eraser of sorts; you can also use clear lemon extract). And add any dabs of bright color in areas you think need a boost. Sprinkle light blue disco dust on some of the light blue areas and purple disco dust on the purple areas. Mix the gold dust with vodka using a small paintbrush to create a thick paint. Splatter gold randomly around the cake.

8   If topping with a sugar flower, use a small dry paintbrush to dust the edges of the flower with bright pink petal dust. Put the white candy melts in a small microwave-safe bowl or ramekin, and microwave in 20-second intervals, stirring well, until melted. Transfer to a small plastic zip-top bag and cut a small hole in one of the corners. Take a grape-size piece of the reserved white fondant and roll it into a ball with your hands. Squeeze a small amount of the melted coating where you want to secure your flower. Press the ball of fondant on top of the coating and press to secure. Add another squeeze of coating and carefully press your flower to secure it. Hold in place until it begins to set, about 1 minute.

9   The cake will keep at cool room temperature for up to 24 hours, and then refrigerated for up to 3 days.

NOTE: Depending on the cake design, I find it's often better to stack the cake tiers prior to decorating. With this cake, I chose to do it that way so that I could work on the three tiers as one canvas, rather than three separate ones. If you would rather paint each cake tier separately and then stack the finished cakes afterwards, that would work just fine as well.

WOW FACTOR WITH NOW FACTOR

For a time-effective finishing touch to any cake, purchase a handmade white sugar flower from a cake-decorating supply shop (see Sources, page 203), and customize it with petal or luster dust before attaching the flower to the cake.

BEADS & BAUBLES CAKE

MAKES ABOUT
18 SERVINGS

Inspired by turquoise beads and baubles, this cake technique is a unique marriage of simplicity and intricacy. The beading effect is easy to create with the use of fondant, gum paste, and a pearl mold. It is rather time-consuming, but the results can be stunning. A quick and simple coral-colored sugar "brooch" adds a retro touch and vibrant punch. I've opted for a lacquered effect to mimic strings of vintage baubles, but you could use a more classic pearl shade for the beads and paint on a pearlescent shimmer. Make the flower brooch a day early so that it has enough time to dry.

1¼ pounds (570 g) white gum paste (I use Satin Ice brand)

AmeriColor gel paste food colors in Soft Pink, Electric Orange, Turquoise, and Mint Green

Confectioners' sugar, for dusting

2 ounces (60 g) candy coating in orange

2 recipes Best-Ever Buttermilk Cake batter (page 151)

2 recipes Swiss Meringue Buttercream (page 176), flavored as desired

3¾ pounds (1¾ kg) white ready-to-use fondant

Instant Edible Varnish (page 200)

Pink gumball

1   Make the brooch flower: Tint 4 ounces (120 g) of gum paste bright coral using equal parts Soft Pink and Electric Orange gel paste color. When not in use, keep the gum paste in a plastic zip-top bag. Using about one-third of the tinted gum paste at a time, roll the paste on a confectioners' sugar–dusted surface to 1/16 inch, and cut the tear shapes out for the petals. Place one petal at a time in the palm of your hand and use the ball of your thumb to rub the center of the petal in a circular motion to create a dip in the petal. Further form the curve of the petals by placing them in a small bowl, using the curve of the bowl for shape. Repeat this until you have at least 6 larger petals and 3 smaller petals (I like to create a few extra in case of breakage). Let dry completely, at least 6 hours.

2   Once dry, arrange the petals in your desired way, overlapping the bottom tips of the petals, and placing the 3 smaller petals in the center. Melt about 1 ounce (30 g) orange candy coating in a small bowl in the microwave and transfer to a small plastic zip-top bag. Cut a small hole in one corner of the bag and squeeze a dab of the "glue" where each petal tip overlaps. Hold down with your finger to help set. Repeat until you have assembled all of the petals. Put the flower in a small bowl. Use another dab of "glue" to adhere the gumball to the center of the flower. Let dry at least 12 hours.

3   Preheat the oven to 350°F (180°C). Grease the bottoms of four 7 × 2-inch and three 5 × 2-inch round cake pans and line with parchment.

RECIPE CONTINUES

TOOLS

2½ × 2-inch and 2 × 2-inch teardrop cutters

5-inch and 7-inch round thin cake boards

Cake-decorating turntable

Nonslip squares

14 mm food-grade silicone pearl mold (see Sources, page 203)

Artist's palette knife

Shortening

Food-safe paintbrushes

Veiner tool (optional)

¼-inch wooden dowels

9- or 10-inch cake drum or platter

NOTE: If you want to create a more realistic pearl look, you can buy smaller pearl molds and replace the edible varnish with a mixture of pearl luster dust mixed with a bit of vodka.

4   Divide the cake batter among the prepared cake pans. Bake two pans in the center of the oven until a wooden pick inserted in the center comes out with a few crumbs, 20 to 22 minutes. Repeat with the final layers. Let the cakes cool in the pans on wire racks for 10 minutes. Run a knife around the edges to loosen, and carefully turn the layers out onto wire racks. Peel off the paper, and let cool completely.

5   Fill and frost both tiers of the cake with the buttercream on the coordinating round thin cake boards and prepare them for covering with fondant (see page 135 for instructions). Refrigerate until firm, about 1 hour.

6   Meanwhile, tint the fondant a vintage turquoise shade using about 15 drops of Turquoise and 3 drops of Mint Green gel paste color. Once you are pleased with the color, divide the fondant as follows and seal each in a plastic zip-top bag: 1 pound plus 8 ounces (680 g) for the 7-inch tier, 1 pound plus 4 ounces (570 g) for the 5-inch tier, and 1 pound (455 g) for the gum paste.

7   The beads are made with a 50-50 mixture of fondant and gum paste. Knead together 1 pound of the turquoise fondant with the remaining white gum paste, adding another 5 drops of Turquoise and 1 drop of Mint Green and kneading until the color is completely blended. Seal in a plastic zip-top bag and set aside.

8   Cover the cake tiers with fondant (see page 139 for instructions). Refrigerate for 1 hour.

9   Prepare a turntable by placing a large nonslip square on top, followed by a piece of wax paper, then a nonslip square (smaller than your cake board). Remove the bottom tier from the refrigerator and place it on the turntable.

10 Dust the inside of a pearl mold with confectioners' sugar and tap out the excess. Take a small amount of the 50-50 mixture, dab a small dot of turquoise gel paste on it, and knead just slightly to create a marbled effect. Fill the mold by pressing the 50-50 firmly into each crevice and overfilling so you have excess 50-50 all along the surface. Run your artist's palette knife flat along the length of the mold to trim the excess. Return it to the plastic zip-top bag to keep it soft. Use your fingers with a tiny dab of shortening to soften any rough edges or stray bits of 50-50. Freeze the mold for about 60 seconds, and then invert it over a work surface. Slowly peel the mold back with one hand

RECIPE CONTINUES

while putting pressure atop the mold with your finger, following along the length of the mold as you pull it back, releasing each part of the bead string. Remember to lift the mold—never try to pull the beads out. Gently pull the string of beads apart so you have two shorter strings (this makes it easier to apply to the cake, as the long strand tends to break apart once lifted).

11 Using a small paintbrush, paint a thin coat of water on the cake only where you will be applying the strand of beads, and then gently press the beads to the cake, taking care to keep them straight. Use the small end of your veiner tool (if using) to gently press down any stray bits of 50-50 at the joins. Repeat these steps until you have gone all the way around the cake. When you apply the strands above each line of adhered beads, be sure to offset the strands slightly, so the actual beads fit into the small open spaces below (like a puzzle) and no cake shows underneath. Refrigerate the beaded cake.

12 Remove the top tier from the fridge and repeat the process, covering the entire cake with beads. Refrigerate for at least 1 hour.

13 Dowel and stack the cake (see page 142 for instructions) onto a cake drum. Refrigerate the assembled cake for at least 1 hour.

14 Remove the chilled cake from the fridge and let any condensation dry. Secure the brooch flower to the top tier of the cake: Melt the remaining ounce (30 g) of orange candy coating and place a dime-size dab of the coating on the underside of the flower and press firmly against the cake until set, about 1 minute. For extra support, insert a few pearl head pins into the cake under the flower to hold the weight until set. Using a medium paintbrush, apply the edible varnish to the entire cake, ensuring that you get into all the nooks and crannies. Let dry for at least 30 minutes. Repeat with a second coat.

15 The cake will keep at cool room temperature for up to 24 hours, and then refrigerated for up to 3 days.

cakelets
IN THE KITCHEN
Let kids paint on the edible varnish! I know it might seem unnerving handing over your masterpiece to tiny persons armed with a paintbrush, but in this case it works. They will have so much fun feeling like fine artists and cake designers, and this frees you up to move on to the next task or do the cleanup (or have a glass of much-deserved wine).

PASTEL PARTY CAKE

MAKES ABOUT 30 SERVINGS

This pastel buttercream and chocolate cake confection celebrates three of my favorite things: sprinkles, pastel colors, and buttercream. Super-moist and decadent dark chocolate cake makes an ideal choice for stacked cakes that need to spend quite a bit of time in the refrigerator, and sprinkly vanilla filling adds a dose of sweet. The trio of birthday-cake-style pastel buttercream tiers is fancy enough for weddings or special parties, and charming enough for anything in between.

2 recipes Simple & Splendid Chocolate Cake batter (page 152)

1 recipe Vanilla Bakery Frosting (page 180), sprinkle variation

2 recipes Swiss Meringue Buttercream (page 176),

AmeriColor gel paste food colors in Soft Pink and Turquoise

½ cup (75 g) rainbow jimmies

TOOLS

Nonslip squares

Cake-decorating turntable

5-inch, 7-inch, and 9-inch round thin cake boards

Pastry brush

Small offset palette knife

Pastry bag

Decorating tip #1M

Pastry comb

¼-inch wooden cake dowels

12-inch cake drum

1 Preheat the oven to 350°F (180°C). Grease the bottoms of three 5 × 2-inch, three 7 × 2-inch, and three 8 × 2-inch round cake pans and line with parchment.

2 Divide the batter among the prepared cake pans. Bake two pans in the center of the oven until a wooden pick inserted in the center comes out with a few crumbs, 20 to 25 minutes. Repeat with the final layers. Let the cakes cool in the pans on wire racks for 10 minutes. Run a knife around the edges to loosen, and carefully turn the layers out onto wire racks. Peel off the paper, and let cool completely.

3 Put a piece of nonslip square on a turntable, followed by a piece of wax paper and then another nonslip square (smaller than your cake board). Put a 9-inch cake board on top and put one of the 8-inch cake layers on it, top up. Brush away any stray crumbs using a dry pastry brush. Using a small offset palette knife, spread about 1 cup of the sprinkle frosting on top. Gently place another 8-inch cake layer on top and repeat. Place the final 8-inch layer on top, bottom up. Wrap the cake tightly in plastic wrap and refrigerate for at least 15 minutes.

4 Repeat the previous step with the 7-inch and 5-inch cakes, but this time using about ¾ cup of sprinkle frosting for each of the 7-inch filling layers, and about ¼ cup for each of the 5-inch layers. Wrap each cake tightly in plastic wrap and refrigerate for at least 15 minutes.

5 Meanwhile, tint about 7 cups of the Swiss buttercream pastel pink using a few drops of Soft Pink gel paste color. Tint about 3 cups of the buttercream pastel turquoise using a few drops of Turquoise gel paste color.

RECIPE CONTINUES

6   Replace the wax paper on the turntable with a fresh piece. Remove the chilled 8-inch cake from the refrigerator, discard the plastic wrap, and put it on the turntable. Frost the cake with a smooth layer of the pink buttercream (see page 135 for instructions), leaving ½ inch of the cake board exposed around the perimeter (this will leave room for the piped buttercream). Refrigerate until firm to the touch, about 1 hour.

7   Replace the wax paper and frost the 7-inch cake using the turquoise buttercream, and the 5-inch cake using the pink buttercream. Refrigerate those cakes until firm to the touch, about 1 hour.

8   Remove the 8-inch cake from the refrigerator, and put it back on the turntable. Fill a large pastry bag fitted with decorating tip #1M one-half full with the pink buttercream. Starting from the bottom of the cake, pipe a rope pattern all around and up the sides of the cake: Press the tip of the pastry bag gently against the cake at a 45-degree angle to the right, apply steady pressure and create a sideways "S" curve shape, dragging just to the right, release. Pull the tip away from the cake and tuck the tip under the bottom of the "S" curve shape just piped. Repeat the same motion until you have gone all of the way around the cake. When piping the next row above your rope, offset the first "S" so it fits into the existing rope like a puzzle. Try counting the same number of seconds with each "S" for accuracy. Repeat until you have reached the top of the cake. Refrigerate for at least 1 hour.

9   Remove the 7-inch cake from the refrigerator, and put it back on the turntable. Frost the cake with another smooth layer of turquoise buttercream. Hold a pastry comb steady at a 45-degree angle against the side of the cake and slowly rotate the turntable until you have gone all the way around. Refrigerate for at least 1 hour.

10 Fold the rainbow jimmies into the remaining pink buttercream. Remove the 5-inch cake from the refrigerator, and put it back on the turntable. Frost the cake with a smooth layer of the sprinkled buttercream. Refrigerate for at least 1 hour.

11 Dowel and stack the cakes (see page 142 for instructions) onto your cake drum.

12 The cake will keep at cool room temperature for up to 24 hours, and then refrigerated for up to 3 days.

PEPPERMINTY DREAM CAKE

MAKES ABOUT
20 SERVINGS

My cakelets and I have decided that if we could bake a cake for Cindy Lou Who, this would be it: a simple but stunning minty vanilla two-tier confection made from moist vanilla cake filled with white chocolate ganache, crushed candy canes, and peppermint whipped cream frosting, and then frosted in sweet, fluffy vanilla frosting. And just for the Who of it, we pipe whimsical poofs of swirled peppermint marshmallow frosting on top. I'm certain this cake would make even the Grinch's heart flutter.

---

1 recipe Pastel Vanilla
Birthday Cake batter
(page 78)

2 recipes Vanilla Bakery
Frosting (page 180)

AmeriColor gel paste food
colors in Soft Pink and
Super Red

1 recipe Chocolate Ganache
(page 190), white chocolate
variation, cooled slightly

½ cup (115 g) crushed classic
red and white candy canes

1 recipe Whipped Cream
Frosting (page 185),
peppermint variation

24 mini candy canes

1 recipe Marshmallow
Frosting (page 173),
peppermint variation

1. Preheat the oven to 350°F (180°C). Grease the bottoms of two 6 × 2-inch and three 8 × 2-inch round cake pans and line with parchment.

2. Divide the batter among the prepared cake pans. Bake two pans in the center of the oven until a wooden pick inserted in the center comes out with a few crumbs, 20 to 25 minutes. Repeat with the final layers. Let the cakes cool in the pans on wire racks for 10 minutes. Run a knife around the edges to loosen, and carefully turn the layers out onto wire racks. Peel off the paper, and let cool completely.

3. Tint the vanilla frosting light pink using a drop or two of Soft Pink gel paste. Set frosting aside. Using a serrated knife, trim any golden crust off the top or sides of all of the cake layers.

4. Put a piece of nonslip square on a turntable, followed by a piece of wax paper and another nonslip square (smaller than your cake board). Put an 8-inch cake board on top and put one of the 8-inch cake layers, top side up, on top, and brush away any stray crumbs using a dry pastry brush. Fit a pastry bag with a large round decorating tip and fill it two-thirds full with the white chocolate ganache (see page 131 for instructions). Pipe a border around the perimeter of the cake layer to create a dam. Using a small offset palette knife, spread about 1 cup of the ganache inside the dam. Sprinkle with a thin layer of crushed candy canes. Using a clean small offset palette knife, spread about 1 cup of the whipped cream frosting over the ganache. Gently place another 8-inch cake layer on top (top side up) and repeat the layers of ganache, candy, and frosting. Place the final 8-inch layer on top, bottom up. Wrap the cake tightly in plastic wrap and refrigerate for at least 1 hour.

5. Meanwhile, repeat the previous step with the 6-inch cake layers.

TOOLS

Long serrated knife

Nonslip squares

Cake-decorating turntable

6-inch and 8-inch round thin cake boards

Pastry brush

3 pastry bags

3 decorating tips #1A

2 small offset palette knives

Medium straight palette knife

¼-inch wooden dowels

10-inch cake drum or platter

Small food-safe paintbrush

6 Replace the wax paper on the turntable with a fresh piece. Remove the chilled 8-inch cake from the refrigerator, discard the plastic wrap, and put it on the turntable. Frost the cake with the pink frosting (see page 135 for instructions), using a straight palette knife to create texture. Refrigerate the cake for at least 1 hour. Repeat this step with the 6-inch cake, and refrigerate for least 1 hour.

7 Dowel and stack the cake (see page 142 for instructions) onto a cake drum or platter.

8 Fit a large pastry bag with a large round tip, and fold the top of the bag over a few inches to form a cuff. Put a few drops of the Super Red gel paste color in a ramekin, and using a paintbrush, paint three evenly spaced lines inside the bag. Fill the bag two-thirds full with the marshmallow frosting (see page 131 for instructions). Holding the pastry bag at a 90-degree angle above the top of the cake, pipe large swirls by gently applying pressure for a few seconds, releasing, and then lifting the pastry bag straight up. If you need to refill the pastry bag, use a clean bag and tip and paint the inside of the bag with the red color in the same manner you did the first time. Gently press the mini candy canes along the bottom of the cake, creating hearts all of the way around.

9 The cake will keep at cool room temperature for up to 8 hours, and then refrigerated for up to 2 days.

DOODLES & DAYDREAMS CAKE

MAKES 26 SERVINGS

I still remember the school days of daydreaming in class, sketching little flowers, cakes, and other random cuteness on anything in my reach. I think you can learn a lot about a person by what they doodle—it's a peek into their world. This cake lets everyone express themselves and share in the fun of decorating. To add to the visual impact of the high-contrast black, white, and rainbow–illustrated fondant, I use decadent black-as-ink velvet cake inside, paired with a duo of vibrantly colored buttercream fillings. Let us daydream; let us doodle!

2 recipes Red Velvet Cake batter (page 157), black velvet variation

3 recipes Swiss Meringue Buttercream (page 176)

AmeriColor gel paste food colors in Regal Purple and Electric Blue

3½ pounds (1¾ kg) white ready-to-use fondant (I prefer Satin Ice brand)

TOOLS

Nonslip squares

4-inch, 6-inch, and 8-inch round thin cake boards

Small offset spatula

¼-inch wooden cake dowels

10-inch round cake drum or platter

Edible food markers (I like AmeriColor)

NOTE: If you find your markers start to lose ink while doodling, simply press the tips firmly onto a paper towel and continue doodling.

1 Preheat the oven to 350°F (180°C). Grease the bottoms of three 4 × 2-inch, three 6 × 2-inch, and four 8 × 2-inch round cake pans and line with parchment.

2 Divide the cake batter among the prepared cake pans. Bake two 8-inch pans in the center of the oven until a wooden pick inserted in the center comes out with a few crumbs, 20 to 25 minutes. Repeat with the final two 8-inch pans. Bake the 4-inch and 6-inch pans three at a time. Let the cakes cool in the pans on wire racks for 10 minutes. Run a knife around the edges to loosen, and carefully turn the layers out onto wire racks. Peel off the paper, and let cool completely.

3 Tint 3 cups of the buttercream purple and 2 cups bright blue. Using a small offset spatula, fill the four 8-inch and three 6-inch and 4-inch tiers of cake with the tinted buttercream on the coordinating round thin cake boards (the 8-inch tier will have 2 layers of purple buttercream). Frost the outside of the cake tiers with the untinted buttercream, working to create a very smooth and even finish for covering with fondant (see page 135 for instructions).

4 Cover each cake tier in the white fondant (see page 139 for instructions), using 1 pound plus 8 ounces (680 g) for the 8-inch tier, 1 pound (455 g) for the 6-inch tier, and 14 ounces (400 g) for the 4-inch tier. Refrigerate the cakes for at least 1 hour.

5 Dowel and stack the tiers (see page 142 for instructions) onto a cake drum or platter. Refrigerate until firm and the fondant is dry, about 2 hours.

6 Remove the cake from the refrigerator and doodle your heart out using a black edible-ink marker. If the fondant becomes sticky from condensation, let it dry before doodling. Let the black ink dry, about 2 hours.

VARIATION: To make a candy-colored, single-tiered version (as on the cover) make 1 recipe of the black velvet cake and 1 recipe Swiss Meringue Bettercream, and use only pink, blue, yellow, and purple food markers.

7 Color in the doodles using bright edible-ink markers, or let guests (or kids) color in the outlines on the tiered cakes or their own slice. Doodling on the entire cake is best done while the cake is cold and firm.

8 The cake will keep at cool room temperature for up to 24 hours, and refrigerated for up to 3 days.

ESSENTIAL BAKING & DECORATING
TECHNIQUES

TIPS FOR SUCCESFUL
BAKING & CAKING

· · · · · · · · · · · · · · ·

HOW TO PREPARE AND
FILL A PASTRY BAG

· · · · · · · · · · · · · · ·

HOW TO OUTLINE
AND FILL IN A COOKIE
WITH ROYAL ICING

· · · · · · · · · · · · · · ·

HOW TO TORTE, FILL,
AND FROST A CAKE

· · · · · · · · · · · · · · ·

HOW TO COVER A CAKE
WITH FONDANT

· · · · · · · · · · · · · · ·

HOW TO DOWEL
AND STACK A CAKE

· · · · · · · · · · · · · · ·

HOW TO TEMPER
CHOCOLATE

· · · · · · · · · · · · · · ·

TIPS FOR SUCCESSFUL BAKING & CAKING

BAKING CAKES

- Always use room-temperature ingredients, unless otherwise instructed in a recipe.

- Use an oven thermometer to ensure that your oven is indeed the proper temperature.

- Bake cakes layer by layer: For example, if you are baking an 8-inch, three-layer cake, split the batter evenly among three 8 × 2-inch round cake pans, rather than baking one taller cake to later be torted. This will ensure even, moist layers.

- Never open the oven door before your cake has started to set, typically at about the 20-minute mark.

- If your cake or cupcakes are domed when they come out of the oven, use the bottom of a cake pan or piece of parchment paper to gently press the top of the cake while it's still hot—presto!

BAKING CUPCAKES

- Most of the same tips apply to baking cupcakes as to baking cakes, but here are a few more cupcake-specific tips and tricks:

- Bake perfectly even cupcakes by using a 3-tablespoon (45 ml) capacity cookie scoop to divide the batter.

- If the tops of your cupcakes tend to dome or aim for the sky when baked, there is a good chance that your oven is much too hot. Again, an oven thermometer is key!

- To prevent the cupcake liners from peeling away after baking, always use greaseproof cupcake liners and be sure that you don't under-bake the cupcakes. Also, never store the cooled cupcakes in an airtight container, as the moisture can cause the liners to peel.

WORKING WITH COLOR

- For best results, use a quality concentrated gel paste food color in all of your cakes and confections (unless otherwise specified in a recipe).

- Always do a small test sample when coloring frostings or fondant, especially when you are combining colors.

- Always tint your frosting in natural light, as indoor lighting can really throw off how the color appears.

- Remember that when the frosting has a slight buttery tone to it (which is impossible to avoid when using butter), the final color will be affected—blues will have a slight turquoise tint, pinks will often have a slightly peachy tint, and so on. I find that a pin dot of violet can help counteract the golden tone. You can also add a few tablespoons of the AmeriColor Bright White soft gel paste color to your batch of frosting to help whiten it (this does help, but unfortunately it isn't the fix-all and tends to cause a slightly odd taste if too much is used). If true colors are imperative, opt for a stark white frosting base, such as white fondant, marshmallow frosting, or royal icing.

- Typically, the color of frosting will become slightly darker after it sits for a bit, so keep this in mind when tinting. Tinted fondant, however, seems to fade as it sits (pink being the most prone to fading).

- Candy clay colors do not fade, even after a long period of time.

- When adding gel paste food color to cake batter, note that the cake will bake very close to the color of your batter—there is minimal color fading when in the oven.

- While fondant takes to color beautifully, too much color can start to break down the fondant, and the excessive kneading will likely cause many unwelcome air bubbles. If you need pitch-black or vibrant red, buy pre-colored fondant.

HOW TO PREPARE AND FILL A PASTRY BAG

YOU WILL NEED:

Pastry bag

Coupler (for standard decorating tips)

Decorating tip

Rubber band

Large glass

1 If using a standard-size decorating tip with a coupler, push the larger piece of the coupler down into the bag (narrow end first) as far as you can, until you feel some resistance (don't force it). Snip the tip of the bag just enough to push the coupler so the threaded portion is exposed. (If you are using a reusable pastry bag, you will only need to cut the tip of the bag the first time.) Place your decorating tip on top and screw the ring onto the coupler tightly (try to catch some of the pastry bag in the ring). Your decorating tip should be nice and stable, with no wiggling (A).

If you are using a large decorating tip, you don't need to use a coupler. Simply drop the tip down into the empty bag, narrow end first, pushing it far enough that the pastry bag fits snugly around it.

2 To fill the bag with royal icing for outlining and flooding, place the prepared pastry bag, tip end down, in a glass, and turn the top of the bag over a few inches to create a cuff over the rim of the glass (B). For other frosting, fillings, or thicker royal icing, you won't need to use a glass—simply hold the bag in one hand with the cuff turned over a few inches.

CONTINUES

A

B

C

3 Fill the bag with no more than about 1 cup of royal icing for piping, or two-thirds full for other frostings and fillings. Pull up the cuff of the bag and gently squeeze upward, pushing out any excess air bubbles. Twist the bag securely, starting where the icing ends, and secure with a rubber band (see C, page 131).

CAKE: FRIEND OR FOE?

Oh, guys. Please don't let my fluffy words in this book imply that there haven't been many failures and frustrations along the way—and that there won't be a few trillion more. You wouldn't believe how many times I have actually cried over cake—cake disasters, minor fails, epic fails, and more. No one is exempt from cake stress; sometimes they simply don't work out. As my friend Vanessa says, "Aliens did it." I think she's on to something. So, let's not be so hard on ourselves. The truth is that there's always someone happy to gobble up the mistakes, and you've likely learned from them. Just keep going—you've got this.

HOW TO OUTLINE AND FILL IN A COOKIE WITH ROYAL ICING

One of the most important details when it comes to decorating cookies with royal icing is the icing's consistency. There are two common ways among cookie decorators to manage this. Some people use two separate bags for each icing color—one for the thicker consistency needed for outlining and another bag with a thinned-out consistency for filling in the cookie. A neat trick I learned from Marian at Sweetopia is to get the icing to a "10-second" consistency (see below), which is a magical in-between consistency that allows you to outline and fill the cookie using the same icing. The key is not to thin past the 10-second consistency or your icing will run right over the outline.

YOU WILL NEED:

Royal Icing (page 194)

Gel paste food color (optional)

Baked and cooled cookies

Pastry bag

Coupler

Decorating tip #2 or #3

Toothpicks

1 **For 10-Second Consistency:** If you are coloring the icing, add a few drops of gel paste food color before you add any water to the icing. Stir to combine, and then add water a few drops at a time until a line made in your icing with the tip of a knife flows back together and disappears in 10 seconds—no more, no less. Always reserve a cup or so of frosting in case you accidentally over-thin it, so you can add a bit more of the original to thicken it up again.

2 **Fill the Pastry Bag:** Prepare a pastry bag with a coupler and a small round tip (either #2 or #3), and fill it with icing (see page 131 for instructions). Brace the wrist of your dominant hand to stabilize your piping and give you much more control. Position your dominant hand in a way that is comfortable and natural for you; I like to hold it like a pen. Practice your piping on a piece of wax paper.

3 **Outline the Cookies:** The outline becomes a dam to hold the rest of the icing while also defining the edge and shape. Be patient; it does take practice. Place a completely cooled cookie on a piece of wax paper, hold the pastry bag over the cookie at about a 45-degree angle, and start applying just enough pressure to outline the shape of the cookie as close to the edge as possible (see A, page 134). Go around the entire shape of the cookie. Use a toothpick to gently ensure that the icing connects and to fix any areas in which the icing threatens to fall off the sides.

CONTINUES

4 Fill in the Cookies: You can either let the outlines dry slightly or fill them right away. If you leave them to dry before filling them, you will have a more pronounced outline; if you fill them right away, you will get more of a seamless look. Beginning at one corner, squeeze the icing onto the cookie, moving back and forth in horizontal lines until you cover the cookie. The icing will start to spread out on its own; use a toothpick to help guide some of the icing that isn't moving as quickly and to move it into the corners (B). Pop any air bubbles with a pin or toothpick. Let dry for at least 4 hours before doing any additional decorating. Let dry for at least 12 hours before wrapping in cellophane bags, and at least 24 hours before you stack the cookies or pack them up to transport.

HOW TO TORTE, FILL, AND FROST A CAKE

This is one of the most valuable skills you will learn when it comes to caking. While there are countless techniques out there, this is exactly how I do it. As with most cake-decorating techniques, you might eventually modify these steps—the most important thing is that you find the way that works for you.

YOU WILL NEED:

Your cake layers, baked and cooled completely

Nonslip squares

Cake-decorating turntable

Thin cake board or cake plate

Long serrated knife

Small offset palette knife

Pastry brush

Medium straight palette knife

Bench scraper

Rectangular metal pan (of any kind)

NOTE: I once read a neat tip from Martha Stewart about "thinking straight" when you're trying to cut something in a straight line. This really works! Every time I torte a cake, I focus on thinking straight, and it makes a huge difference— no wonky layers. (This also works well when cutting gift wrap, craft paper, or pretty much anything at all!)

1 **Prepare the Cake Layers:** Wrap the cake layers in plastic wrap and freeze for 15 minutes, or refrigerate for 30 minutes. Put a large (but smaller than the diameter of your turntable) nonslip square on the turntable, followed by a large piece of wax paper, and then a nonslip square smaller than the diameter of your cake. Put a cake board on top and spread a small dollop of frosting in the center.

2 Using a long serrated knife, trim the tops of the cakes flat and trim off any dark crust along the sides of the layers, if needed. Discard the crusts and be sure your workspace is crumb-free. Place the first cake layer, top up, on the cake board (A).

3 **Torte the Cake Layers:** *Torting* is slicing thick cake layers in half horizontally in order to make twice as many thin layers. There are countless gadgets designed to torte cakes evenly, but honestly, I find using a good serrated knife gives you the most control and works like a charm. Hold a serrated knife in your dominant hand and gently place the palm of your other hand on top of the cake.

CONTINUES

A

B

NOTE: If your frosting loses its "spreadability," employ this quick and easy fix: Put a butter-based frosting in a heatproof bowl and microwave in 10-second intervals, stirring in between, until it is soft and spreadable. For a confectioners' sugar–based frosting that has just been made but has a lot of air bubbles in it, use a rubber spatula to beat some of the air out of it with an aggressive back-and-forth paddling motion.

4   Crouch down to get a better perspective, and put the knife blade at the halfway point on the side of the cake. Begin slicing into the cake in a gentle sawing motion and use your other hand to start rotating the cake. Continue this motion until you have gone all the way around and can feel the cake has disconnected into two separate layers (see B, page 135). You can also torte the layers on a piece of wax paper on a counter. Let your knuckles rest on the counter surface—that way you are holding your knife at the same height while you are slicing all the way around the cake.

5   Voilà! You have officially torted a cake.

6   **Fill the Cake:** The frosting itself is key here—its consistency is crucial, as you need the frosting to be as smooth and creamy as possible (see Note). The more "glide" it has, the more beautifully it will move around the cake with no resistance.

      A general rule of thumb for filling cakes is that the frosting thickness should be equal to about half the thickness of the cake layers. So, if your cake layers are 2 inches high, then the filling should be about 1 inch thick.

      If you are frosting the outside of the cake in the same frosting, you can extend the frosting over the edge of the cake. But if you are using a different color or different frosting for the outside, keep the filling layer about ½ inch from the edge (C).

7   Place a large dollop of frosting on the first cake layer and use the small offset palette knife to spread into an even later. Repeat until you come to the final layer. When you come to the final cake layer, put it on bottom up so that the top of your cake will be as flat as possible (D).

8   For cakes with fillings that ooze (such as citrus curd, fruit compotes, etc.), you'll want to take an extra step. Before spreading the filling over each layer, fit a pastry bag with a

C

D

NOTE: Crumb-coating might just be the secret that frustrated home bakers never take the time to do. Essentially, you are applying a "base coat" of frosting that seals in all of the crumbs before you apply a fresh coat of frosting for show. You aren't going for perfection here, but you do want to achieve a uniform layer of frosting over the entire cake.

large round decorating tip (such as #1A) and fill it two-thirds full with the thicker frosting to be used on the outside of the cake (see page 131 for instructions). Pipe a dam of frosting around the perimeter of each cake layer, and then spread the filling inside. This keeps that oozy filling goodness inside, rather than squishing out the sides of the cake when you add layers on top of it.

9 Once your final layer is on top, take a look at the cake from above, as this is the best way to see if the layers are lined up. Cover the entire cake with a snug layer of plastic wrap. Use your hands to press on the plastic wrap and then wiggle the cake layers into place, if needed. Refrigerate the cake (on the turntable, if you have room in your fridge) for 30 minutes, or as otherwise instructed in your recipe.

10 **Crumb-Coating the Cake:** Remove the cake from the refrigerator and discard the plastic wrap. Put the cake back on the turntable. Brush away any stray crumbs using a pastry brush. Top the cake with a very large dollop of frosting, and using a small offset palette knife, spread the frosting over the cake, extending it over the edge all around (E).

11 Switch to a medium straight palette knife and, beginning at the top, spread out the excess frosting that is extending over the sides. Working top down and in small sections (a few inches by a few inches), generously apply frosting until it just adheres to the cake, gently spreading it in a back-and-forth motion. The key is to use as much frosting as possible so your palette knife never really comes in contact with the cake itself (F).

12 Use a bench scraper to smooth the sides: With your dominant hand, hold your bench scraper still and snugly right up against the side of the cake, and use your other hand to slowly rotate the

CONTINUES

E

F

G

turntable. Use your small offset palette knife to pull the excess frosting onto the top of the cake and do your best to smooth the top with your palette knife. (G)

13 Refrigerate the cake until the frosting is no longer sticky to the touch, 20 to 30 minutes.

14 **Add the Show Coat:** Next, you put on the show coat, which makes a smooth buttercream finish. Remove the cake from the refrigerator, and begin to frost the cake in the same manner as you did for the crumb-coat stage. Before you smooth the frosting edges over the top of the cake, fill a rectangular metal pan (one big enough to hold your small offset spatula and medium straight spatula) with very hot water, and put your decorating tools in it.

15 Pull the small offset spatula out of the water, dry it, and use it to smooth the frosting over the top of the cake, dipping your spatula back into the hot water and drying it after each smoothing motion. Crouch down to eye level to check for an even top surface. Remove the straight spatula from the water, dry it, and use it to smooth out any rough areas on the sides of the cake. Pull any additional frosting over the top if necessary using your offset spatula. Continue with this process until you are pleased with how it looks.

16 **Optional Fondant Coating:** You can either be done at this point or you can proceed to prepare the cake for covering in fondant (opposite). It is really important that your frosting has no lumps, bumps, or cake showing through. Refrigerate the cake until it is extremely firm, at least 1 hour.

HOW TO COVER A CAKE WITH FONDANT

For the first dozen or more times that I covered a cake in fondant, I literally broke a sweat because I was so nervous. But then I realized that it really wasn't so bad, and that it was only my fear that was holding me back. So once I got some practice behind me, I discovered that fondant isn't so scary. Actually, once you get the hang of it, it's like the sweet skies open up and anything is possible in the land of fancy cake.

YOU WILL NEED:

Ready-to-use fondant

Gel paste food color (optional)

Fondant mat (optional)

Your chilled (and very firm) frosted cake

Large rolling pin

Straight pin

Fondant smoothers

Pizza cutter

Cake pan about 2 inches smaller than the diameter of your cake

Small sharp kitchen knife

Shortening

Small piece of acetate (about 4 inches square)

1   Weigh out the required quantity of fondant for your cake. If you are tinting your fondant, add a few drops of gel paste food color and knead until you are pleased with the color. Immediately seal the fondant in a plastic zip-top bag.

2   Put the fondant mat, if using, on a work surface. Put a large piece of wax paper beside the mat. Remove the chilled cake from the refrigerator and put it on the wax paper. (If you aren't using a fondant mat, dust the clean surface with confectioners' sugar to avoid sticking.) Remove the fondant from the bag, and knead it on the mat until it is smooth and pliable, about 30 seconds. Press the fondant into a flat disc.

3   Using a large rolling pin, roll the fondant from the center out (not back and forth as you'd roll a pie crust), working your way around the fondant (A, page 140). Roll the fondant to ¼-inch thickness and the dimensions you need (see Note, page 140), working quickly, as the fondant will dry out, which can result in small cracks once it's on the cake.

4   Use a pin to pop any air bubbles in the fondant as you go.

5   Using the rolling pin, carefully lift the fondant and unroll it on top of the cake (see B, page 140).

6   Use the fondant smoother to smooth out any air pockets on the top of the cake, and quickly press the top edges of the fondant around the cake—this minimizes the weight of the fondant, which will help to avoid tears (see C, page 140).

7   Working quickly but gently, use your fingertips and the palm of your hand to flatten the fondant around the cake, gradually working your way down to the bottom (see D, page 140). Once

CONTINUES

NOTE: Here's a basic formula to calculate the amount of fondant for a cake: height of the cake × 2 + diameter = total amount needed. So, for example, if you have an 8-inch round cake that is 4 inches high, it's 4 × 2 = 8 + 8 = 16. You then know you need a circle of fondant that is at least 16 inches in diameter. You will want a little extra to be safe, so add 2 inches. You don't want too much excess fondant, or the weight of it will cause it to tear when you apply it to the cake.

you get to the bottom, trim any of the excess fondant with a pizza cutter, leaving about an extra inch of overhang.

8   Using fondant smoothers, smooth the fondant from the top out and down (E). Lift the cake onto the upside-down cake pan (E), and using a small sharp knife, trim the excess.

9   Smooth out any rough edges along the bottom using your finger dipped in a bit of shortening. Continue smoothing and perfecting your fondant by gently rubbing an acetate square over the cake (you can even use a flattened ball of fondant) (F). Use a paper towel with a dab of shortening to repair minor nicks, dryness, or other small imperfections—simply rub in a gentle circular motion over the imperfection to add moisture and buff the imperfection out.

10   Refrigerate the cake until about 6 to 8 hours before serving.

11   You can cover a cake in fondant up to about 3 days in advance. The fondant seals all of the moisture into the cake, keeping it surprisingly fresh and moist for several days.

A   B   C

D   E   F

A FEW MORE NOTES ON FONDANT

MORE TIPS

- To soften fondant, add shortening and knead until soft and pliable.

- Water is the enemy when working with fondant—even a drop of water will dissolve it, resulting in a sticky, gooey mess. If you do get a small amount of water on your fondant, knead in a finger-full of shortening.

- If you want to dry out sticky fondant, sprinkle a little confectioners' sugar or cornstarch on it. To avoid tackiness in humid weather, use a pastry brush to dust cornstarch or confectioners' sugar on the finished fondant cake.

- Fondant attracts fibers, so try to wear white while working with it, if possible. If you do see small fibers or other specks on your fondant, remove them with a straight pin and then smooth over.

- Give fondant-covered cakes a pleasant sheen by buffing with a small amount of shortening on a paper towel (it's best to do this when the cake is firm).

- When cutting decorative shapes out of fondant, sprinkle a generous amount of confectioners' sugar or cornstarch on your work surface before cutting. Let the shapes dry out for about 15 minutes before handling them or adhering them to your desserts.

NOTE: When I'm covering a cake in fondant, I always use a meringue-based buttercream (Italian or Swiss) because it creates a very stable base that will hold up to the weight of the fondant, and it firms up rock-hard (think very cold butter).

CAKING TIMELINE

Here's the timing I follow for a Saturday fancy-cake delivery: I make the buttercream (Swiss or Italian) up to one month ahead of time and freeze it. Tuesday before delivery, I pull the buttercream from the freezer and let it thaw on the counter overnight. I bake the cakes early on Wednesday and let them cool completely before wrapping them in plastic wrap and leaving them at room temperature. Later that same day, I fill and frost the cakes, getting them ready for covering with fondant. Wednesday evening, I cover the cakes with fondant and let them chill overnight. I spend Thursday and Friday working on the cake decorating, putting the cakes in and out of the refrigerator during that time so they don't get overly soft.

One thing I've learned is to never leave any decorating to the day of delivery—ever. What a nightmare that can be if things don't go the way you envisioned, or if something else happens and you run out of time. Eek!

SHOULD YOU REFRIGERATE A FONDANT-COVERED CAKE?

Many people debate whether or not fondant-covered cakes should go in the fridge. Yes, indeed, they can. As a matter of fact, they need to. I put my fondant-covered cakes in and out of the refrigerator countless times during a single cake decorating session if the cake begins to soften while I'm working on it.

The thing is, fondant doesn't like moisture, but it's necessary (especially in warmer environments) to chill the cake to prepare for decorating. If you try to decorate a soft fondant-covered cake, you will end up with bumps and indents in your fondant, and it just doesn't look appealing. Fondant condensation (aka sweat) will evaporate once it's in a cool, dry environment again. (To speed up this process, you can use an electric fan.)

HOW TO DOWEL AND STACK A CAKE

When stacking a cake—even if it's simply a small-scale two-tier cake—you need to add stability to the base cake so that it can carry the weight of whatever you put on it. The larger, and therefore heavier, the cake to be placed on top, the more dowels you need to put in the bottom cake to support it.

You might have heard of cake decorators using plastic drinking straws for support, as well as thicker plastic dowel rods, but I prefer wooden dowels because they are sturdy but slender. When I'm stacking a buttercream cake, I insert an additional dowel that goes straight down through the center of the top tier and gets pushed through the entire cake, creating a very stable structure—just so the buttercream cakes don't shift.

YOU WILL NEED:

Chilled cakes on thin cake boards

¼-inch wooden dowels (I like Wilton)

Fine marker

Sharp shears (I use garden shears)

Royal Icing (page 194)

Cake drum

Long ¼-inch-thick wooden dowel rod the height of the stacked cake

Clean pencil sharpener

Hammer

1 **Dowel the Cakes:** Outline the shape of the tier to be placed on top by centering a cake pan or cake board of the same size and shape onto the center of the cake, gently pressing down, and giving it a little twist to leave an imprint (A). If you're working with a fondant-covered cake and the fondant is hard, outline the shape with tiny pin marks.

2 Calculate how many dowels you will need—you will be evenly spacing them about 1½ inches in from the outline, and I find odd numbers work well.

3 Insert one of the short wooden dowels into the cake, pushing straight down until you feel the cake board below (B). Mark the dowel where it meets the cake with a marker or sharp knife (C) and remove the dowel. Wipe the dowel clean and, using the shears, cut

A

B

C

D

it about ⅛ inch shorter than your mark. Cut the remaining dowels to the length of the cut dowel (D).

4 Insert the dowels one at a time, using the shape of the outline as your guide. Be sure to press straight down until you hit the cake board. Repeat these steps with all additional tiers except the top tier.

5 **Stack the Cakes:** Spread or pipe about 1 tablespoon of stiff-peak royal icing on the center of the cake drum, and put the bottom tier on the center of the drum. If you are using fondant-covered cakes, spread about 1 tablespoon of stiff-peak royal icing into a thin layer in the center of your dowels.

6 Center the next tier and carefully drop it onto the cake below, and gently wiggle it into place with your hands (if fondant), or use an offset spatula to gently shift it into place (E, F).

7 Repeat until you have stacked all of the cake tiers.

CONTINUES

E

F

8 **Stake the Cakes:** For buttercream cakes, or if you feel that your fondant cake needs extra support, you stake the cake. Hold a long wooden dowel beside the stacked cakes and cut the length of your dowel about 1 inch shorter than the total height of the cake. Sharpen one end with a clean pencil sharpener until very sharp, and stand on a step stool so you are directly above the cake.

9 Hold the dowel directly over the center of the top tier, and insert it straight down about an inch or so. Use your dominant hand to hold the hammer and the other hand to hold the dowel steady, and begin to hammer the dowel straight down—you will feel when you hit the cake boards, but the sharp point of the dowel will pierce the cake board and continue through to the next tier. Keep hammering until your dowel is flush with the top of your cake. Use your finger to carefully push the tip of the dowel further into the cake so it is no longer visible.

10 Cover the hole by spreading a touch of buttercream over it, or press a tiny pad of fondant on top. Decorate the cake and refrigerate it.

11 **Consider Some Finishing Touches:** Some minimalist designs leave the borders of the cake tiers untouched so that you can see the seams, but if you like a seamless look for your stacked cakes, you can easily fill those gaps. Fit a small pastry bag with a coupler and small round tip, and then fill with a small amount of royal icing tinted the same color as your fondant (just note that the icing will dry about a half shade darker than the color when it is wet). Pipe a small bit of icing along the seam. Use a damp finger or food-safe paintbrush to smooth the frosting.

HOW TO TEMPER CHOCOLATE

To achieve the shininess and snap that all good molded chocolate treats have, you have to temper the chocolate. After trying many different and more complicated tempering methods, I learned a super-simple controlled-melting microwave method that works like a dream—it hasn't failed me yet!

For successful tempering with this method, it's best to use at least 7 ounces (200 g) of chocolate. I use Callebaut chocolate callets because they are a premium chocolate that is readily available at baking supply shops and is ideal for tempering. This method works for any type of chocolate: dark, milk, or white; however, milk and white chocolate will temper more quickly.

YOU WILL NEED:

Microwave-safe plastic bowl

Instant read thermometer (I like Thermapen)

Put the chocolate in a microwave-safe plastic bowl (if working with bar chocolate, chop it first). Microwave at full power for 1 minute. Stir the chocolate well and microwave for 20 more seconds. Remove and stir for about 30 seconds. There should still be some visible pieces of unmelted chocolate, which will melt once stirred well. If there are still chocolate pieces that will not melt by stirring, microwave in 5- to 10-second intervals and stir again until smooth, but be sure the chocolate does not heat over 90°F (32°C) for dark chocolate, 86°F (30°C) for milk chocolate, and 84°F (29°C) for white chocolate. Voilà! Your chocolate is now tempered and ready to create gorgeous, snappy, shiny treats.

THE SHOW MUST GO ON

If your chocolate does go past the ideal temperature, it is important that you add about 20 percent more stable solid chocolate pieces to bring the temperature down, and not simply try to cool the chocolate down by refrigerating it or letting it sit.

PRIZED
BASIC CAKE RECIPES

SUPER WHITE CAKE

. . . .

BEST-EVER
BUTTERMILK CAKE

. . . .

SIMPLE & SPLENDID
CHOCOLATE CAKE

. . . .

CHOCOLATE
BUTTER CAKE

. . . .

BLUEBERRY CAKE

. . . .

RED VELVET CAKE

. . . .

PINK CHERRY CAKE

. . . .

SUPER WHITE CAKE

MAKES THREE 8-INCH ROUND LAYERS

Lofty, moist, white, and fluffy—this vanilla white cake is the best I've ever made. I find this cake to be very consistent. For me, this is what brings me back to those supermarket bakery cake days, and I adore it. It's a crowd-pleaser—kids and adults love it the same. Extremely versatile, it pairs well with pretty much any type of frosting, or you can serve it warm from the oven with a sprinkling of confectioners' sugar. For a double-dose of childhood bliss, pair this cake with the Vanilla Bakery Frosting (page 180) and create the Pastel Party Cake (page 121).

3¼ cups (375 g) cake flour, sifted

1 tablespoon plus 1 teaspoon baking powder

¾ teaspoon salt

2¼ cups (450 g) superfine sugar

¾ cup (170 g) cold unsalted butter, cut into pieces

1½ cups (360 ml) milk, room temperature

2 teaspoons Princess Bakery Emulsion (see Note) or pure vanilla extract

1 teaspoon fresh lemon juice

7 large egg whites, room temperature

1 Preheat the oven to 350°F (180°C). Grease the bottoms of three 8 × 2-inch round cake pans and line with parchment.

2 Into the bowl of an electric mixer fitted with the paddle attachment, sift together the flour, baking powder, and salt. Add the sugar. With the mixer running on low speed, add the cold butter one piece at a time. Beat until all of the butter is incorporated, about 3 minutes. The mixture should have a fine crumbly, cornmeal-like texture.

3 In a medium measuring cup with a spout, combine half the milk, the emulsion, and lemon juice. In a separate measuring cup, gently whisk the egg whites and remaining milk.

4 Increase the mixer speed to medium-low and gradually add the emulsion mixture and beat for 5 minutes. Scrape the sides and bottom of the bowl with a rubber spatula. Reduce the mixer speed to low and gradually add the egg white mixture. Beat for 2 minutes, occasionally stopping to scrape the sides and bottom of the bowl. Fold the batter once or twice to ensure everything has been incorporated. Divide the batter evenly among the prepared pans.

5 Bake the first two layers in the center of the oven until a wooden pick inserted into the center comes out with a few crumbs, 20 to 22 minutes. Repeat with the final layer. Let the cake layers cool in their pans on wire racks for 10 minutes. Using a knife, loosen the sides of the cakes and carefully turn them out onto wire racks. Peel off the paper liners and let cool completely.

6 The cake layers will keep wrapped tightly in plastic wrap at room temperature for up to 2 days.

NOTE: The first time I tried the Princess Bakery Emulsion from LorAnn Oils in my vanilla cakes and cookies, I was hooked. The sweet vanilla and slightly lemony taste brings me right back to my childhood, and I love that the flavor doesn't bake away in the oven, the way vanilla extract can. That being said, a quality pure vanilla extract will add a subtler, and possibly more authentic, vanilla flavor to this cake.

NOTE: The sugars in vanilla cake often cause a deep golden "crust" all over the cake. For a picture-perfect frosted vanilla cake, trim all of the sides and tops of the layers with a serrated knife before assembling and frosting the cake.

A NOTE ABOUT BAKING PANS

The prized basic cakes in this chapter are designed to be baked in three 8 × 2-inch round pans. The layers are each about 1½ inches high (this varies slightly), which makes for impressive layer cakes once filled and frosted. Alternatively, you can bake these cake recipes in the following:

- Two 9-inch round cake pans, for 28 to 30 minutes

- Three 7-inch round cake pans, for 22 to 26 minutes

- One baker's half-sheet pan (18 × 13 × 1 inch), for 18 to 22 minutes

- One 9 × 13-inch pan, for 30 to 35 minutes

- 2 to 3 dozen cupcake liners, for 17 to 20 minutes

- 12 jumbo cupcake liners, for 22 to 25 minutes

BEST-EVER BUTTERMILK CAKE

MAKES THREE 8-INCH ROUND LAYERS

I can still vividly recall my mom serving yellow buttermilk cake at our family birthday dinners during the late 1970s and early 1980s—complete with the glass rectangular baking pan, smothered in what I imagine was Duncan Hines chocolate frosting and topped with randomly tossed silver dragées. This yellow buttermilk cake is impossibly moist and has a beautiful vanilla bean flavor that pairs wonderfully with the cake's buttery texture (try this cake warm out of the oven with a sprinkling of confectioners' sugar—a cakey dream). Pair these layers with anything from sweet frostings and fillings to the darkest of chocolate—I love the silky Chocolate Cloud Frosting (page 179) or the super-dark Glossy Fudge Frosting (page 187). Also try the Swiss Meringue Buttercream (page 176), as I did in the showstopping Love & Butter Cake (page 99).

3 cups (345 g) cake flour, sifted

2 cups (410 g) superfine sugar

1 tablespoon plus 1 teaspoon baking powder

¾ teaspoon salt

1 cup (225 g) cold unsalted butter, cut into pieces

1 cup (240 ml) buttermilk, room temperature

2 teaspoons vanilla bean paste or pure vanilla extract, or seeds from ½ vanilla bean

5 large eggs, room temperature

1 Preheat the oven to 350°F (180°C). Grease the bottoms of three 8 × 2-inch round cake pans and line with parchment.

2 In the bowl of an electric mixer fitted with the paddle attachment, whisk together the flour, sugar, baking powder, and salt. With the mixer running on low speed, add the cold butter one piece at a time. Beat until all of the butter is incorporated, about 3 minutes. The mixture should have a fine crumbly, cornmeal-like texture.

3 In a medium measuring cup with a spout, combine half of the buttermilk and the vanilla bean paste. In a separate measuring cup, gently whisk the eggs and remaining buttermilk.

4 Increase the mixer speed to medium-low. Gradually add the vanilla mixture and beat for 5 minutes. Scrape the sides and bottom of the bowl with a rubber spatula. Reduce the mixer speed to low and gradually add the egg mixture in three additions, scraping the sides of the bowl after each addition. Beat until well combined, 2 minutes. Fold the batter once or twice to ensure everything has been incorporated. Divide the batter evenly among the prepared pans.

5 Bake the first two layers in the center of the oven until a wooden pick inserted into the center comes out with a few crumbs, 20 to 22 minutes. Repeat with the final layer. Let the cake layers cool in their pans on wire racks for 10 minutes. Using a knife, loosen the sides of the cakes and carefully turn them out onto wire racks. Peel off the paper liners and let cool completely.

6 The cake layers will keep wrapped tightly in plastic wrap at room temperature for up to 3 days.

SIMPLE & SPLENDID CHOCOLATE CAKE

MAKES THREE 8-INCH ROUND LAYERS

What this cake should really be called is "the supercalifragilisticexpialidocious chocolate cake." Seriously. If there's ever been a cake that is super-quick and simple to make, bakes up like a dream, tastes divine and chocolaty beyond words, and pleases a crowd, it is this one. It is extremely versatile, and although it pairs well with anything from salted caramel to raspberry buttercream, it can stand on its own as more of a teatime cake dusted with confectioners' sugar.

You'll notice I use this cake in many forms throughout the book—layer cakes, fondant-covered cakes, baked in a sheet pan, and mini cakes—as it bakes well in any size or shape. Go for an old-fashioned-meets-rainbow sprinkles cupcake with the Sky-High Chocolate-Covered Cupcakes (page 25), or maybe a towering chocolate cake is more your style, like the Cloud 9 Cake (page 93)?

2½ cups (320 g) all-purpose flour

2½ cups (520 g) superfine sugar

1 cup (120 g) best-quality Dutch-process dark cocoa powder (I like Cacao Barry Extra Brute)

2 teaspoons baking soda

2 teaspoons baking powder

1 teaspoon salt

1½ cups (360 ml) buttermilk

1 cup (240 ml) hot coffee or espresso

¾ cup (180 ml) vegetable oil

3 large eggs, room temperature

1 tablespoon pure vanilla extract

1 Preheat the oven to 350°F (180°C). Grease the bottoms of three 8 × 2-inch round cake pans and line with parchment.

2 Into the bowl of an electric mixer fitted with the whisk attachment, sift the flour, sugar, cocoa powder, baking soda, baking powder, and salt. In a large measuring glass with a spout, whisk together the buttermilk, coffee, oil, eggs, and vanilla. With the mixer running on low speed, gradually add the milk mixture and beat until smooth, about 1 minute. Use a rubber spatula to scrape the sides and bottom of the bowl. Divide the batter evenly among the prepared pans.

3 Bake the first two layers in the center of the oven until a wooden pick inserted into the center comes out with a few crumbs, 20 to 25 minutes. Repeat with the final layer. Let the cake layers cool in their pans on wire racks for 10 minutes. Using a knife, loosen the sides of the cakes and carefully turn them out onto wire racks. Peel off the papers and let cool completely.

4 The cake layers will keep wrapped tightly in plastic wrap at room temperature for up to 3 days.

CHOCOLATE BUTTER CAKE

MAKES THREE 8-INCH ROUND LAYERS

While I love the ease, simplicity, depth, and darkness of the oil-based Simple & Splendid Chocolate Cake (page 152), there is something magical about a dark chocolate butter cake.

2⅓ cups (315 g) all-purpose flour

1 cup (120 g) best-quality Dutch-process dark cocoa powder (I use Cacao Barry Extra Brute)

1½ teaspoons baking powder

¾ teaspoon salt

1½ cups (360 ml) buttermilk, room temperature

½ cup (120 ml) hot coffee

1 cup (225 g) unsalted butter, room temperature

2½ cups (560 g) packed light brown sugar

2 teaspoons pure vanilla extract

4 large eggs, room temperature

¼ cup (60 g) mayonnaise, room temperature

1½ teaspoons baking soda

2 teaspoons distilled white vinegar

1 Preheat the oven to 350°F (180°C). Grease the bottoms of three 8 × 2-inch round cake pans and line with parchment.

2 In a large bowl, whisk together the flour, cocoa powder, baking powder, and salt. In a large measuring glass with a spout, combine the buttermilk and coffee. Set aside.

3 In the bowl of an electric mixer fitted with the paddle attachment, beat the butter and brown sugar on medium speed until very light and fluffy, about 8 minutes. Add the vanilla and beat well. Add the eggs one at a time, mixing well and scraping the sides of the bowl with a rubber spatula after each addition.

4 Remove the bowl from the mixer, and using a rubber spatula, fold in one-third of the flour mixture until just combined. Add half of the buttermilk mixture and fold until just combined. Repeat with the remaining flour and buttermilk mixtures. Fold in the mayonnaise.

5 In a small bowl, whisk together the baking soda and vinegar, and quickly fold into the batter. Don't over-mix. Divide the batter evenly among the prepared pans.

6 Bake the first two layers in the center of the oven until a wooden pick inserted into the center comes out with a few crumbs, 20 to 25 minutes. Repeat with the final layer. Let the cake layers cool in their pans on wire racks for 10 minutes. Using a knife, loosen the sides of the cakes and carefully turn them out onto wire racks. Peel off the papers and let cool completely.

7 The cake layers will keep wrapped tightly in plastic wrap at room temperature for up to 3 days.

VARIATIONS

- **Chocolate Root Beer Cake:** Omit the coffee and the vanilla extract. Reduce the brown sugar to 2 cups (445 g) and the buttermilk to ½ cup (120 ml). Add ¾ teaspoon root beer flavor oil or 2 teaspoons root beer extract in place of the vanilla, and add 1 can (355 ml) root beer (not diet) to the buttermilk in step 2.

BLUEBERRY CAKE

MAKES THREE 8-INCH ROUND LAYERS

This ultra-moist cake is visually stunning with its bursts of blueberries throughout. For fun, I've added a turquoise hue to the batter, but that can certainly be left out. Tossing the blueberries in a quick coat of flour keeps them from sinking to the bottom. This cake pairs incredibly well with lemon, lavender, vanilla, and many other flavors.

3¾ cups (430 g) cake flour, sifted, plus more for berries

1 tablespoon baking powder

¾ teaspoon salt

1 cup plus 5 tablespoons (300 g) unsalted butter, room temperature

2¼ cups (460 g) superfine sugar

2 teaspoons pure vanilla extract or Princess Bakery Emulsion (see Note, page 148)

1 teaspoon fresh lemon juice, plus more for wiping bowl

2 or 3 drops AmeriColor gel paste food color in Turquoise (optional)

5 large eggs, separated, room temperature

2 cups (480 ml) milk, room temperature

1½ cups (250 g) wild blueberries, fresh or frozen

1 Preheat the oven to 350°F (180°C). Grease the bottoms of three 8 × 2-inch round cake pans and line with parchment.

2 In a large bowl, whisk together the flour, baking powder, and salt.

3 In the bowl of an electric mixer fitted with the paddle attachment, beat the butter and 1¾ cups of the sugar on medium speed until very light and fluffy, about 8 minutes. Add the vanilla, lemon juice, and gel paste (if using) and beat well. Add the egg yolks two at a time, mixing well after each addition and scraping the sides of the bowl with a rubber spatula. Reduce the mixer speed to the lowest speed, and add one-third of the flour mixture until just combined. Add half of the milk and mix until just combined. Repeat until all of the flour mixture and milk have been incorporated and the batter is smooth (do not over-mix).

4 Wipe the inside of a stainless mixer bowl with a little lemon juice. Put the egg whites in the bowl, fit the mixer with the whisk attachment, and beat on medium speed while gradually adding the remaining ½ cup sugar. Increase the mixer speed to medium-high and beat until medium peaks form, 1 to 2 minutes. Fold the egg whites into the batter until incorporated (do not over-mix).

5 Toss the blueberries with a little flour and fold them into the batter. Divide the batter evenly among the prepared pans.

6 Bake two pans in the center of the oven until a wooden pick inserted into the center comes out with a few crumbs, 25 to 30 minutes. Repeat with the final layer. Let the cake layers cool in their pans on wire racks for 10 minutes. Using a knife, loosen the sides of the cakes and carefully turn them out onto wire racks. Peel off the papers and let cool completely.

7 The cake layers will keep wrapped tightly in plastic wrap at room temperature for up to 2 days.

RED VELVET CAKE

I have to admit that it took me a while to grow fond of red velvet cake, but when I fell, I fell hard. Its scarlet crumb is enchanting, but I think it was the taste that did me in—the most tender, moist buttermilk cake with a slightly tangy flavor and hint of chocolate.

I like to dazzle this cake whenever possible, as I did with the Red Velvet Cakelets (page 28) and the sparkly Sprinkle Twinkle Cake (page 112). Fancy stuff aside, this cake is just as delightful paired with a classic Fluffy Cream Cheese Frosting (page 183) or Vanilla Bakery Frosting (page 180).

3 cups (345 g) cake flour, sifted

1 teaspoon baking powder

1 teaspoon Dutch-process dark cocoa powder

¾ teaspoon salt

½ cup (115 g) unsalted butter, room temperature

2 cups (410 g) superfine sugar

½ cup (120 ml) vegetable oil

2 tablespoons Red Velvet Bakery Emulsion (see Note)

3 large eggs, room temperature

1½ cups (360 ml) buttermilk, room temperature

1 teaspoon baking soda

2 teaspoons distilled white vinegar

NOTE: The Red Velvet Bakery Emulsion from LorAnn Oils adds a gorgeous deep red hue and subtle citrus flavor that make this cake unique and tasty. But don't worry if you can't get your hands on any—this cake recipe is still dynamite the old-fashioned way: add 1 tablespoon pure vanilla extract plus 3 tablespoons red liquid food coloring in place of the emulsion.

1 Preheat the oven to 350°F (180°C). Grease the bottoms of three 8 × 2-inch round cake pans and line with parchment.

2 In a large bowl, whisk together the flour, baking powder, cocoa powder, and salt. Set aside.

3 In the bowl of an electric mixer fitted with the paddle attachment, beat the butter, sugar, oil, and emulsion on medium speed until very light and fluffy, 5 to 7 minutes. Add the eggs one at a time, mixing for 20 seconds and scraping the sides of the bowl with a rubber spatula after each addition. Reduce the mixer speed to low and add one-third of the flour mixture until just combined. Add half the buttermilk and mix until just combined. Repeat until all of the flour mixture and buttermilk have been added.

4 In a small bowl, combine the baking soda and vinegar, and quickly whisk it into the batter. Divide the batter evenly among the prepared pans.

5 Bake two pans in the center of the oven until a wooden pick inserted into the center comes out with a few crumbs, 20 to 25 minutes. Repeat with the final layer. Let the cake layers cool in their pans on wire racks for 10 minutes. Using a knife, loosen the sides of the cakes and carefully turn them out onto wire racks. Peel off the papers and let cool completely.

6 The cake layers will keep wrapped tightly in plastic wrap at room temperature for up to 2 days.

VARIATION

- **Black Velvet Cake:** Add 2 teaspoons AmeriColor gel paste food color in Super Black with the emulsion.

PINK CHERRY CAKE

MAKES THREE 8-INCH ROUND LAYERS

Every time I bake this cake I feel a sudden desire to wear a pink 1950s dress and a polka-dot apron. Its retro charm and delightfulness are timeless. Add a hint of pink gel paste for an extra-pretty finish. This cake pairs well with almost any flavor—anything vanilla, almond, or even chocolate (give it a try with the Neapolita Cake on page 90).

3¼ cups (375 g) cake flour, plus more for cherries

2¼ cups (450 g) superfine sugar

1 tablespoon plus 1 teaspoon baking powder

½ teaspoon salt

¾ cup (170 g) cold unsalted butter, cut into pieces

1⅓ cups (320 ml) milk, room temperature

2 tablespoons Maraschino cherry juice

1 teaspoon fresh lemon juice

1 teaspoon pure vanilla extract or Princess Bakery Emulsion (see Note, page 148)

7 large egg whites, room temperature

1 or 2 drops AmeriColor gel paste food color in Soft Pink (optional)

About 20 (100 g) Maraschino cherries, chopped

1 Preheat the oven to 350°F (180°C). Grease the bottoms of three 8 × 2-inch round cake pans and line with parchment.

2 In the bowl of an electric mixer fitted with the paddle attachment, combine the flour, sugar, baking powder, and salt on low speed. Add the butter one piece at a time. Beat on low speed until all the butter has been incorporated, about 3 minutes. The mixture should have a fine crumbly, cornmeal-like texture.

3 In a medium measuring glass with a spout, combine half the milk, the cherry juice, lemon juice, and vanilla. In a separate measuring cup, gently whisk the egg whites and remaining milk.

4 With the electric mixer running on low speed, gradually add the cherry juice mixture, followed by the gel paste color (if using), and beat for 5 minutes. Scrape the sides and bottom of the bowl with a rubber spatula. Put the electric mixer back on low speed and add the egg white mixture in three parts, scraping down the sides of the bowl after each addition. Beat for 1 minute. Toss the cherry bits in a little flour and gently fold them into the batter (do not over-mix). Divide the batter evenly among the prepared pans.

5 Bake two pans in the center of the oven until a wooden pick inserted into the center comes out with a few crumbs, 20 to 25 minutes. Repeat with the final layer. Let the cake layers cool in their pans on wire racks for 10 minutes. Using a knife, loosen the sides of the cakes and carefully turn them out onto wire racks. Peel off the papers and let cool completely.

6 The cake layers will keep wrapped tightly in plastic wrap at room temperature for up to 2 days.

CUTOUT COOKIES
FOR DECORATING

GINGERY GINGERBREAD
CUTOUT COOKIES

· · · · · · · · · · · · · · ·

VANILLA SUGAR
CUTOUT COOKIES

· · · · · · · · · · · · · · ·

DARK CHOCOLATE SUGAR
CUTOUT COOKIES

· · · · · · · · · · · · · · ·

BLACK VELVET SUGAR
CUTOUT COOKIES

· · · · · · · · · · · · · · ·

GINGERY GINGERBREAD CUTOUT COOKIES

MAKES ABOUT 24 MEDIUM COOKIES

My little 7-year-old Reese is a gingerbread fanatic. This still surprises me greatly, considering she is particular in her food choices. For this recipe, we both felt that we should really celebrate the spices and flavor, and kick it up a notch. So our version is just sweet and spicy enough to make them extremely addictive and memorable.

3⅓ cups (450 g) all-purpose flour, plus more for dusting

2 teaspoons ground ginger

2 teaspoons ground cinnamon

¼ teaspoon ground allspice

½ teaspoon baking soda

½ teaspoon salt

¾ cup (170 g) unsalted butter, room temperature

¾ cup (170 g) packed light brown sugar

1 large egg, lightly beaten

⅔ cup (240 g) cooking molasses (see Note)

1 teaspoon pure vanilla extract

NOTE: For a milder molasses flavor, use "fancy" or unsulphured molasses. For a more robust (and darker brown) cookie, use cooking molasses.

1 In a large bowl, whisk together the flour, ginger, cinnamon, allspice, baking soda, and salt.

2 In the bowl of an electric mixer fitted with the paddle attachment, cream the butter and brown sugar on medium speed until it becomes a pale paste (you don't want it to be super-fluffy, or the cookies will expand when baking), about 2 minutes. Add the egg and beat well. Add the molasses and vanilla and beat well. Reduce the mixer speed to the lowest setting, and gradually add the flour mixture, beating until just incorporated (do not over-mix). Wrap the ball of dough in plastic wrap, and press it into a disc. Refrigerate for 1 hour.

3 Put a large piece of parchment on a work surface and sprinkle with flour. Unwrap the chilled dough and put it on the parchment. Put two ¼-inch wooden dowels on either side of the dough and sprinkle the top of the dough with a little flour. Put a second sheet of parchment on top. Roll out the dough until it's flush with the dowels. If the dough is sticking, add a bit more flour. Slide the parchment and dough onto a board and freeze for at least 15 minutes.

4 Preheat the oven to 350°F (180°C). Line two baking sheets with silicone baking mats or parchment. Remove the dough from the freezer, and cut out shapes using the cutters of your choice. Put the shapes about 1½ inches apart on the prepared baking sheets. Freeze for 15 minutes.

5 Bake the cookies until the edges are just crisp but not dark brown, 12 to 14 minutes, depending on the size of your cookies. Let the cookies cool on the baking sheets on wire racks for 10 minutes. Gently transfer the cookies to wire racks to cool completely.

6 The cookies will keep in an airtight container at room temperature for up to 2 weeks, or in the freezer for up to 2 months.

VANILLA SUGAR CUTOUT COOKIES

MAKES ABOUT 30 MEDIUM COOKIES

These buttery cookies have crisp, light golden edges and semi-soft centers, and to me they are the ultimate vanilla sugar cookie. By not over-beating the butter and sugar, you can get away with adding baking powder, which adds a desirable airiness to the inside of each cookie while managing to have the cookies keep their shape while baking. For a bit of sparkle, sprinkle the cookies with sanding sugar before baking.

3½ cups (470 g) all-purpose flour

½ teaspoon baking powder

½ teaspoon salt

1 cup (225 g) unsalted butter, room temperature

1¼ cups (260 g) superfine sugar

2 teaspoons pure vanilla extract or Princess Bakery Emulsion (see Note, page 148)

1 large egg, lightly beaten

3 tablespoons (45 ml) milk

1 In a large bowl, whisk together the flour, baking powder, and salt.

2 In the bowl of an electric mixer fitted with the paddle attachment, beat the butter and sugar on medium speed until it becomes a pale paste (you don't want it to be super-fluffy, or the cookies will expand when baking), 2 minutes. Add the vanilla and beat well. Add the egg and milk and beat until incorporated, about 1 minute. Reduce the mixer speed to the lowest setting, and gradually add the flour mixture, beating until just incorporated (do not over-mix). Wrap the ball of dough in plastic wrap and press it firmly into a disc. Refrigerate for 1 hour.

3 Unwrap the chilled dough and put it on a large piece of parchment. Put two ¼-inch wooden dowels on either side of the dough and put a second piece of parchment paper on top. Roll out the dough until it's level with the dowels. Slide the parchment and dough onto a board and freeze or refrigerate for about 15 minutes.

4 Preheat the oven to 350°F (180°C). Line two baking sheets with silicone baking mats or parchment. Remove the dough from the refrigerator, and cut it into shapes using the cutters of your choice. Put the shapes about 1½ inches apart on the prepared baking sheets. Freeze for at least 15 minutes.

5 Bake the cookies one sheet at a time on the center rack until the edges are just crisp and a very light golden color, 12 to 15 minutes (this can vary greatly, depending on your oven, the size of your cookies, and how long they were in the freezer). Let the cookies cool on the baking sheets on wire racks for 10 minutes. Gently transfer the cookies to wire racks to cool completely.

6 The cookies will keep in an airtight container at room temperature for 1 week, or in the freezer for up to 2 months.

RECIPE CONTINUES

VARIATIONS

- **Almond Sugar Cutout Cookies:** Reduce the vanilla to 1 teaspoon, and add 1 teaspoon pure almond extract.

- **Vanilla Bean Sugar Cutout Cookies:** Replace the vanilla extract with vanilla bean paste or the seeds of ½ vanilla bean.

- **Lemon Sugar Cutout Cookies:** Omit the vanilla and add 1 teaspoon fresh lemon juice and the grated zest of 1 lemon.

- **Lavender Sugar Cutout Cookies:** Add 2 teaspoons culinary lavender to the dry ingredients.

- **Orange Sugar Cutout Cookies:** Omit the vanilla and add ½ teaspoon pure orange extract and 1 tablespoon grated orange zest.

- **Confetti Sugar Cutout Cookies:** Use a wooden spoon to stir in ¼ cup (35 g) confetti quin sprinkles just before you wrap the dough in plastic.

TIPS FOR MAKING PERFECT CUTOUT COOKIES

- If you want to add color to cutout-cookie recipes, add it along with the flavorings, as it will be best incorporated that way.

- Avoid adding excess flour when rolling out your cookie dough, which can dry out and toughen your cookies before you know it. The cutout cookie recipes in this book are designed to not require any extra flour when rolling, with the exception of gingerbread cookie dough, which will require only a small amount. If you find your dough sticks while rolling, try flipping the dough.

- If you like a thicker cookie, use ¼-inch-thick dowels; or use ⅛-inch-thick dowels for thinner cookies. You have a very small window right after the cookies come out of the oven to carefully "push in" any spread edges before they cool, but just remember that they are extremely hot!

- Try to cut as many cookies as you can after rolling the dough. The more you roll and reroll sugar cookie dough, the tougher the baked cookies will be. I recommend rolling the same batch of cookie dough only twice to ensure light, tender cookies.

- Use a small round cutter (or other shape) to use up the extra bits of rolled dough— these make perfect little snack cookies, and cakelets love them!

- To guarantee perfectly shaped cutout cookies, always use the "triple-chill" method: chill the dough before and after rolling, and chill the cookie cutouts before baking.

C IS FOR CREATIVE COOKIE CUTOUTS

You can create any cookie template imaginable by simply drawing a shape onto plain card stock by hand or printing an image from your computer. Use a craft mat and X-Acto craft knife to achieve very precise templates, or simply cut with craft scissors. Place your template on top of any rolled and chilled cutout cookie dough, and cut around the template with a small, sharp knife or X-Acto craft knife.

DARK CHOCOLATE SUGAR CUTOUT COOKIES

MAKES ABOUT 20 MEDIUM COOKIES

From a cookie-decorating perspective, chocolate cutout cookies add an appealing contrast, particularly when covered in pure white or pastel icing. I created this recipe by altering a prize-worthy vanilla cookie recipe. The dark cocoa powder brings such a deep chocolate-ness, and I've added a smidge of espresso powder to heighten the chocolate. I figure if we're going to make chocolate cookies, they need to be really chocolaty cookies.

2¾ cups (350 g) all-purpose flour

¾ cup (90 g) best-quality Dutch-process dark cocoa powder (I use Cacao Barry Extra Brute)

1 teaspoon instant espresso powder (optional)

½ teaspoon baking powder

½ teaspoon salt

1 cup (225 g) unsalted butter, room temperature

1 cup (205 g) superfine sugar

½ cup (110 g) packed light brown sugar

2 tablespoons milk

1 tablespoon pure vanilla extract

1 large egg, lightly beaten

1 In a large bowl, whisk together the flour, cocoa powder, espresso powder (if using), baking powder, and salt.

2 In the bowl of an electric mixer fitted with the paddle attachment, beat the butter and sugars on medium speed until the mixture becomes a pale paste (you don't want it to be super-fluffy, or the cookies will expand when baking), 2 minutes. Add the milk and vanilla, and beat well. Add the egg and beat until incorporated, about 1 minute. Reduce the mixer speed to the lowest setting, and gradually add the flour mixture, beating until just incorporated (do not over-mix). Wrap the ball of dough in plastic wrap, and press it into a disc. Refrigerate for 1 hour.

3 Unwrap the chilled dough and put it on a large piece of parchment. Put two ¼-inch wooden dowels on either side of the dough and put a second sheet of parchment on top. Roll out the dough until it's level with the dowels. Slide the parchment and dough onto a board and freeze or refrigerate for about 15 minutes.

4 Preheat the oven to 350°F (180°C). Line two baking sheets with silicone baking mats or parchment. Remove the dough from the refrigerator, and cut out shapes using the cutters of your choice. Put the shapes about 1½ inches apart on the prepared baking sheets. Freeze for at least 15 minutes.

5 Bake the cookies until the edges are firm and the center is still soft, 12 to 15 minutes (this can vary greatly, depending on your oven, the size of your cookies, and how long they were in the freezer prior to baking). Let the cookies cool on the baking sheets on wire racks for 10 minutes. Gently transfer them to wire racks to cool completely.

6 The cookies will keep in an airtight container at room temperature for up to 1 week, or in the freezer for up to 2 months.

BLACK VELVET SUGAR CUTOUT COOKIES

MAKES ABOUT 30 MEDIUM COOKIES

When I had a vision for the Menagerie Masquerade Cookies (page 69), I felt that the cookies themselves needed to be a little more . . . mysterious. So I set out to create a tasty cookie that would have a deep shade of black. Rather than simply going crazy with the black food color, I thought it would be more of a natural transition to work from the ingredients found in the Black Velvet Cake (variation, page 157). These deep, dark, black-as-night cutout sugar cookies are rich, buttery, and crisp enough to keep their shape while baked, but have a semi-soft center.

4½ cups (520 g) cake flour, sifted

1 tablespoon plus 1 teaspoon Dutch-process dark cocoa powder

½ teaspoon baking powder

½ teaspoon salt

1 cup (225 g) unsalted butter, room temperature

1¼ cups (260 g) superfine sugar

2 teaspoons Red Velvet Bakery Emulsion (see Note, page 157)

1½ teaspoons AmeriColor gel paste food color in Super Black

1 large egg, lightly beaten

2 tablespoons buttermilk

NOTE: If you can't get the Red Velvet flavor emulsion, use 2 teaspoons pure vanilla extract and 1 teaspoon AmeriColor Super Red gel paste color mixed with 2 teaspoons water (in addition to the Super Black gel paste color).

1 In a large bowl, whisk together the flour, cocoa powder, baking powder, and salt.

2 In the bowl of an electric mixer fitted with the paddle attachment, beat the butter and sugar on medium speed until it becomes a pale paste (you don't want it to be super-fluffy, or the cookies will expand when baking), 2 minutes. Add the emulsion and gel paste and beat well. Add the egg and buttermilk, and beat until incorporated, about 1 minute. Reduce the mixer speed to the lowest setting, and gradually add the flour mixture, beating until just incorporated (do not over-mix). Wrap the ball of dough in plastic wrap, and press it into a disc. Refrigerate for 1 hour.

3 Unwrap the chilled dough and put it on a large piece of parchment. Put two ¼-inch wooden dowels on either side of the dough and put a second sheet of parchment on top. Roll out the dough until it's level with the dowels. Slide the parchment and dough onto a board and freeze or refrigerate for about 15 minutes.

4 Preheat the oven to 350°F (180°C). Line two baking sheets with silicone baking mats or parchment. Remove the dough from the refrigerator, and cut out shapes using the cutters of your choice. Put the shapes about 1½ inches apart on the prepared baking sheets. Freeze for at least 15 minutes.

5 Bake the cookies until the edges are just crisp, 12 to 15 minutes (this can vary greatly, depending on your oven, the size of your cookies, and how long they were in the freezer prior to baking). Let the cookies cool on the baking sheets on wire racks for 10 minutes. Gently transfer the cookies to wire racks to cool completely.

6 The cookies will keep in an airtight container at room temperature for 1 week, or in the freezer for up to 2 months.

VARIATION

◄ **Red Velvet Sugar Cookies:** For a more traditional red velvet version, simply omit the black color.

FROSTINGS,
FILLINGS & MORE

MARSHMALLOW FROSTING

· · · · · · · · · · · · · ·

ITALIAN MERINGUE
BUTTERCREAM

· · · · · · · · · · · · · ·

SWISS MERINGUE
BUTTERCREAM

· · · · · · · · · · · · · ·

CHOCOLATE CLOUD FROSTING

· · · · · · · · · · · · · ·

VANILLA BAKERY FROSTING

· · · · · · · · · · · · · ·

FLUFFY CREAM CHEESE
FROSTING

· · · · · · · · · · · · · ·

TOASTED MARSHMALLOW
FROSTING

· · · · · · · · · · · · · ·

WHIPPED CREAM FROSTING

· · · · · · · · · · · · · ·

GLOSSY FUDGE FROSTING

· · · · · · · · · · · · · ·

SHINY CHOCOLATE GLAZE

· · · · · · · · · · · · · ·

CHOCOLATE GANACHE

· · · · · · · · · · · · · ·

SALTED CARAMEL

· · · · · · · · · · · · · ·

ROYAL ICING

· · · · · · · · · · · · · ·

ZINGY CITRUS CURD

· · · · · · · · · · · · · ·

CANDY CLAY

· · · · · · · · · · · · · ·

SIMPLE SYRUP

· · · · · · · · · · · · · ·

INSTANT EDIBLE VARNISH

· · · · · · · · · · · · · ·

CONFECTIONERS' GLAZE

· · · · · · · · · · · · · ·

MARSHMALLOW FROSTING

MAKES ABOUT 4 CUPS

There's nothing like a pure white, divine frosting. I love this billowy frosting because it's one of the only frostings (aside from those that use shortening) that actually is perfectly white and accepts blue, green, and pink colors the way we love.

4 large egg whites

1¼ cups (250 g) granulated sugar

1 tablespoon light corn syrup

¼ teaspoon cream of tartar

Pinch of salt

1 teaspoon pure vanilla extract

1   Wipe the stainless steel bowl and whisk of an electric mixer with a paper towel dampened with a little lemon juice to eliminate any trace of grease. Put the egg whites, sugar, corn syrup, cream of tartar, and salt in the bowl and put it over a saucepan of barely simmering water (be sure the bottom of the bowl is not touching the water). Whisk constantly but gently until the mixture reaches 130°F (54°C), 7 to 9 minutes.

2   Transfer the bowl to the mixer. Beat the mixture on low speed for 2 minutes, then increase the speed to medium and beat for 2 more minutes. Increase the speed to high and beat until it is very thick and glossy, about 5 minutes. Add the vanilla and beat well.

3   The frosting is best used right away, but it will keep covered at room temperature for up to 1 hour.

NOTE: Be sure your sugar–egg white mixture is hot enough to dissolve all the sugar granules, or you will end up with grainy frosting.

VARIATIONS

▪ **Cotton Candy Marshmallow Frosting:** Substitute the sugar with cotton candy sugar and omit the vanilla.

▪ **Peppermint Frosting:** Reduce the vanilla to ½ teaspoon and add ½ teaspoon peppermint extract, or more to taste.

ITALIAN MERINGUE BUTTERCREAM

MAKES 6 CUPS

This luxurious buttercream is almost identical to Swiss Meringue Buttercream (page 176) in its appearance, taste, and texture; however, the method sets them apart. I've included both types because there seems to be an even divide among bakers and cakers as to which they prefer. Whereas Swiss buttercream is prepared by heating the egg whites and sugar before whipping into a meringue, Italian buttercream is prepared by first whipping room-temperature egg whites slightly before adding a sugar syrup made from sugar and water, which lends a stiff-peak, glossy meringue. I have worked with both methods, and while I find the Italian method creates a slightly more creamy and stable buttercream, the difference is marginal. Most times I make the Swiss version because I find the recipe doubles well.

7 large egg whites

¼ teaspoon cream of tartar

1¾ cups (350 g) granulated sugar

⅓ cup (80 ml) water

2 cups (455 g) unsalted butter, room temperature, cut into cubes

2 teaspoons pure vanilla extract or vanilla bean paste

Pinch of salt

1 Wipe the stainless steel bowl and paddle attachment of an electric mixer with a paper towel dampened with a little lemon juice to eliminate any trace of grease. Put the egg whites and cream of tartar in the bowl and put it on the mixer. Beat the mixture on low speed until it is frothy, about 30 seconds. Gradually add ¼ cup sugar. Increase the speed to medium-high and beat until soft peaks form, about 30 more seconds.

2 In a small saucepan set over high heat, heat the remaining 1½ cups sugar and the water until it reaches 180°F (82°C), about 5 minutes. Continue to cook the syrup until it reaches 240°F (115°C), 1 to 2 minutes.

3 Set the mixer speed to high and pour the syrup into the meringue in a thin, steady stream. Beat until the bottom of the bowl has cooled, about 12 minutes. Switch to the paddle attachment, and with the mixer on low speed, add the butter one piece at a time. Increase the speed to medium and beat until the buttercream is thick and fluffy, about 1 minute. Reduce the speed to low, add the vanilla, and salt, and beat for 3 minutes.

4 The buttercream will keep covered at room temperature for 1 day, refrigerated in an airtight container for up to 1 week, or in the freezer for up to 3 months. Bring the buttercream to room temperature when ready to use.

5 To bring buttercream back to a spreadable consistency, microwave one-fourth of the batch for about 10 seconds and put all of the buttercream in the bowl of an electric mixer. Beat on medium speed until it is fluffy and creamy, about 2 minutes.

VARIATIONS

For more ideas, see Swiss Meringue Buttercream, page 176.

- **Caramel Meringue Buttercream:** Add ½ cup (175 g) homemade or store-bought caramel (or salted caramel) to the prepared buttercream and beat well (or you can leave some unblended caramel swirls throughout—yum!).

- **Chocolate Italian Meringue Buttercream:** Add 10 ounces (300 g) best-quality dark or extra-dark chocolate, melted and cooled, to the prepared buttercream and beat until combined.

- **Cookies & Cream Meringue Buttercream:** Beat 6 to 8 crumbled sandwich cookies (such as Oreos) into the prepared buttercream.

- **Fruity Meringue Buttercream:** Add up to ⅓ cup (80 ml) fruit puree—such as raspberry, strawberry, mango, or passionfruit—to the prepared buttercream and beat well.

- **Peanut Butter Meringue Buttercream:** Add about ¾ cup (190 g) smooth peanut butter to the finished buttercream and beat well.

SWISS MERINGUE BUTTERCREAM

MAKES 6 CUPS

Swiss meringue buttercream is the choice for fancy cakes and for preparing a cake for fondant. It pipes like a dream, too. This really is my all-time favorite buttercream when it comes to cake decorating because of its silky texture and rich but not super-sweet taste. Also, it can be doubled easily. This is the ultimate choice for those who are looking for a not-so-sweet buttercream. If you've never made it, it can seem rather intimidating, but once you get the hang of it, you'll be hooked.

7 large egg whites

1¾ cups (350 g) granulated sugar

2 cups (455 g) unsalted butter, room temperature, cut into cubes

2 teaspoons pure vanilla extract or vanilla bean paste, or the seeds of ½ vanilla bean

Pinch of salt

1 Wipe the stainless steel bowl, whisk, and whisk and paddle attachment of an electric mixer with a paper towel dampened with a little lemon juice to eliminate any trace of grease. Add the egg whites and sugar and put the bowl over a pot of simmering water. Cook, whisking constantly but gently, until the temperature reaches 130°F (54°C).

2 Return the bowl to the mixer and fit it with the whisk attachment. Beat on medium-high speed until it reaches the stiff peak stage (very thick and glossy), about 2 minutes. Decrease the speed to medium and beat until the bottom of the bowl is cool, about 10 minutes.

3 Switch to the paddle attachment, and with the mixer running on low speed, add the butter one piece at a time. Beat until the mixture is silky smooth, about 1 minute. Add the vanilla and salt, and beat on low speed for 3 more minutes.

4 The buttercream will keep covered at room temperature for 1 day, refrigerated in an airtight container for up to 1 week, or in the freezer for up to 3 months. Bring the buttercream to room temperature when ready to use (this can take up to 8 to 12 hours).

5 To bring buttercream back to a spreadable consistency, beat on medium-low speed for about 2 minutes. If your buttercream still isn't fluffy, you can microwave about 1 cup of it for about 10 seconds to soften (it's okay if it partially melts), and then add it to the remaining buttercream and beat again.

NOTE: Use fresh egg whites instead of the pasteurized carton variety, as they lead to the most voluminous meringues.

RECIPE CONTINUES

VARIATIONS

For more ideas, see Italian Meringue Buttercream, page 174.

- **Brown Sugar Meringue Buttercream:** Substitute the granulated sugar with brown sugar. You can use either light or dark brown sugar, though the latter will have a more pronounced flavor.

- **Candied Ginger Meringue Buttercream:** Beat ½ cup (55 g) minced crystallized ginger (not in syrup) into the prepared buttercream.

- **Chocolate Swiss Meringue Buttercream:** Beat 9 ounces (270 g) melted and cooled best-quality dark chocolate into the prepared buttercream.

- **Lemon Meringue Buttercream:** Beat up to ½ cup (120 ml) lemon curd (see page 197 for instructions) into the prepared buttercream.

- **Mocha Meringue Buttercream:** Reduce the vanilla to 1 teaspoon. Beat 8 ounces (240 g) melted and cooled best-quality dark chocolate, plus 2 teaspoons instant espresso powder that has been dissolved in 1 tablespoon water, into the prepared buttercream.

- **Strawberry Meringue Buttercream:** Beat up to ⅓ cup (80 ml) strawberry puree into the prepared buttercream. For a boost of pretty pink, add a drop of AmeriColor Soft Pink gel paste color.

- **White Chocolate Meringue Buttercream:** Beat 7 ounces (200 g) melted and cooled best-quality white chocolate (not white chocolate chips) into the prepared buttercream.

CHOCOLATE CLOUD FROSTING

MAKES ABOUT 5 CUPS

This decadent dark chocolate frosting literally whips up like chocolate clouds. The secret is to use the best dark chocolate you can find, which balances out the sweetness of the confectioners' sugar. I use a food processor for this recipe because it lends the silkiest texture and takes only a few moments to make the frosting.

2 cups (455 g) unsalted butter, room temperature

4 cups (500 g) confectioners' sugar, sifted

⅓ cup (80 ml) heavy cream

2 teaspoons pure vanilla extract

¼ teaspoon pure almond extract

Pinch of salt

7 ounces (200 g) best-quality dark chocolate, chopped or callets/discs

1 Put the butter, sugar, cream, vanilla, almond extract, and salt into a food processor and pulse until combined, about 1 minute.

2 Melt the chocolate in the microwave. Add the melted and slightly cooled chocolate to the food processor and blend until smooth, about 1 minute. If the frosting is too soft, simply refrigerate until it firms up slightly, about 10 minutes.

3 For ideal spreading consistency, it is best used right away. The frosting will keep in an airtight container in the refrigerator for up to 3 days. When ready to use, bring it to room temperature and beat on low speed to bring it back to spreadable consistency.

VARIATIONS

- **Malted Chocolate Cloud Frosting:** Omit the almond extract and add ¾ cup (75 g) malt powder (or malted drink mix, such as Milo or Ovaltine) along with the confectioners' sugar.

- **Mocha Cloud Frosting:** Add 2 teaspoons instant espresso powder to the heavy cream, stirring to dissolve.

- **Nutella Cloud Frosting:** Blend 1 cup (240 ml) Nutella into the prepared frosting.

- **Root Beer Cloud Frosting:** Replace the vanilla and almond extracts with 1 teaspoon root beer flavor oil or 2 teaspoons root beer extract.

VANILLA BAKERY FROSTING

MAKES ABOUT 4 CUPS

This frosting is fluffy, sweet, and the most reminiscent of that sugary bakery frosting we find on sprinkled cupcakes and layer cakes in supermarkets. It's also the quintessential birthday cake frosting that many of us cherish from our childhood, making it a crowd-pleasing favorite.

1 cup (225 g) unsalted butter, room temperature

¼ cup (50 g) high-ratio shortening (see Note)

Pinch of salt

3¼ cups (410 g) confectioners' sugar, sifted

½ cup (120 ml) heavy cream

2 teaspoons pure vanilla extract or vanilla bean paste

¼ teaspoon pure almond extract

NOTE: You can certainly use all butter, rather than the high-ratio shortening, if you prefer. High-ratio shortening is used to add stability and tenderness to white cakes and creaminess and stability to frostings. In a pinch you can also use regular shortening, such as Crisco, but the high-ratio version is designed for frosting and gives a much better mouth-feel.

1 In the bowl of an electric mixer fitted with the paddle attachment, beat the butter, shortening, and salt on medium speed until very pale and creamy, 8 minutes. Gradually add the confectioners' sugar, heavy cream, vanilla, and almond extract.

2 Reduce the speed to the lowest setting and beat for 1 minute. Increase the speed to medium-high and beat until very light and fluffy, about 6 minutes.

3 The frosting will keep in an airtight container in the refrigerator for up to 3 days. Bring chilled frosting to room temperature and beat on low speed to soften. If necessary, you can warm the frosting in a heatproof container in the microwave in 10-second intervals, stirring after each one, until smooth and spreadable.

VARIATIONS

- **Cotton Candy Bakery Frosting:** Option 1: Omit the vanilla and the almond extract. Add ½ teaspoon cotton candy flavor oil. Option 2: Beat 1 cup (30 g) packaged cotton candy into the prepared frosting on medium speed.

- **Lavender Bakery Frosting:** Add ¼ teaspoon culinary lavender extract, or to taste. Add a drop each of AmeriColor Violet and Regal Purple gel paste color for a pastel lavender hue, if desired.

- **Lemon Bakery Frosting:** Omit the vanilla, almond extract, and heavy cream. Add 2 tablespoons fresh lemon juice and the grated zest of 1 lemon.

- **Sprinkle Bakery Frosting:** Fold in ½ cup rainbow jimmies and ½ cup confetti quins before using.

- **Stark White Bakery Frosting:** For a pure white version, use ⅔ cup (120 g) high-ratio shortening and ⅓ cup (75 g) butter; increase the confectioners' sugar to 5 cups (625 g); add 2 tablespoons light corn syrup; add ⅓ cup water; and substitute clear imitation vanilla extract for the pure vanilla. Note that this frosting will be a crusting buttercream, which means the surface of the frosting will not stay tacky to the touch—it will develop a slight crust once it is exposed to air.

- **Pink Cherry Bakery Frosting:** Beat in 2 tablespoons chopped Maraschino cherries and 2 tablespoons Maraschino cherry juice.

- **Vanilla Ice Cream Bakery Frosting:** Omit the almond extract and beat in ½ cup (120 ml) melted vanilla ice cream. In a pinch, you can use ½ cup half-and-half.

- **White Chocolate Bakery Frosting:** Beat 6 ounces (170 g) melted and slightly cooled best-quality white chocolate (not white chocolate chips) into the whipped butter and shortening in the middle of step 1. Continue on with step 2, adding an additional tablespoon or so of heavy cream if necessary.

FLUFFY CREAM CHEESE FROSTING

MAKES ABOUT 5 CUPS

Rich, fluffy, and as creamy as can be, this tangy frosting is a perfect addition to almost any cake or cupcake you can dream up. The key to a super-smooth, lump-free cream cheese frosting is to ensure that the cream cheese is very soft and that it is added only after the other ingredients have been well beaten.

1 cup (225 g) unsalted butter, room temperature

3 cups (375 g) confectioners' sugar, sifted

2 teaspoons pure vanilla extract

½ teaspoon fresh lemon juice

Pinch of salt

2 (8-oz/225 g) packages cream cheese, softened and cut into cubes

1 In the bowl of an electric mixer fitted with the paddle attachment, beat the butter on medium speed for 5 minutes. Add the confectioners' sugar, vanilla, lemon juice, and salt; decrease the speed to low and beat for 1 minute.

2 Increase the speed to medium and beat until fluffy, about 4 minutes. Reduce the speed to medium-low, add the cream cheese, and beat until smooth, about 1 minute. (Try not to over-beat at this stage, as the cream cheese will cause the frosting to become very thin.)

3 The frosting will keep covered at room temperature for up to 6 hours, and then refrigerated in an airtight container for up to 3 days. Bring chilled frosting to room temperature and beat on low speed to soften.

VARIATIONS

▪ **Lemon Cream Cheese Frosting:** Reduce the vanilla extract to 1 teaspoon, and increase the lemon juice to 1 tablespoon. Beat the grated zest of 1 lemon into the prepared frosting.

▪ **Lemon & Candied Ginger Cream Cheese Frosting:** Beat ¼ cup (30 g) minced crystallized ginger (not in syrup) into the prepared Lemon Cream Cheese Frosting.

TOASTED MARSHMALLOW FROSTING

MAKES ABOUT 4 CUPS

The secret to making the ultimate toasted marshmallow frosting is adding a batch of homemade vanilla Marshmallow Frosting, rather than using store-bought marshmallow crème. The supreme fluffiness of the marshmallow frosting, along with the crispy bits of charred marshmallows, creamy butter, and sweet confectioners' sugar, creates the best campfire-inspired frosting.

20 large (150 g) white marshmallows (I use Jet-Puffed brand)

¾ cup (170 g) unsalted butter, room temperature

1½ cups (190 g) confectioners' sugar, sifted

1 teaspoon pure vanilla extract or vanilla bean paste

Pinch of salt

1 recipe Marshmallow Frosting (page 173)

1 Preheat the oven to broil. Line a baking sheet with aluminum foil or parchment.

2 Arrange the marshmallows on the prepared sheet in a single layer. Broil the marshmallows, watching closely, until they are toasted and slightly charred, about 3 minutes. Remove the baking sheet from the oven and, using a pair of tongs, carefully turn the marshmallows over. Return the baking sheet to the oven and broil for 1 to 2 minutes more. Remove the baking sheet from the oven and let cool. Using a greased rubber spatula, put the cooled marshmallows into a food processor.

3 In the bowl of an electric mixer fitted with the paddle attachment, beat the butter on medium speed until light and fluffy, about 6 minutes. Reduce the speed to low and gradually add the confectioners' sugar, vanilla, and salt. Increase the speed to medium-high and beat until fluffy, about 3 minutes.

4 Transfer the buttercream to the food processor. Pulse a few times until the marshmallows are dispersed but there are still pieces of toasted marshmallow remaining. Transfer the mixture back to the mixer bowl and beat on medium speed until incorporated, about 30 seconds.

5 Stop the mixer and add the marshmallow frosting. Beat on low speed until combined, but try not to over-beat, as it will deflate some of the marshmallow frosting.

6 The frosting is best used immediately, but it will keep covered at room temperature for up to 1 day.

NOTE: I used to make frosting with toasted marshmallows by adding them straight to the mixer, but I found that by using the food processor, the marshmallows become evenly incorporated and it cuts the final gooey stretchiness factor that using the mixer seems to cause.

WHIPPED CREAM FROSTING

MAKES ABOUT 4 CUPS

Essentially, this is a stabilized whipped cream, so you get all of the simplicity and airiness of fresh whipped cream, but with the ability to withstand the weight of cake layers and time. It can be used as a light and not-so-sweet frosting or filling.

2 tablespoons cold water

2 teaspoons unflavored gelatin (such as Knox)

2 cups (480 ml) heavy cream, cold

½ cup (105 g) superfine sugar

2 teaspoons vanilla bean paste or pure vanilla extract, or seeds from ½ vanilla bean

Pinch of salt

NOTE: The keys to success are to be sure that your gelatin mixture is cool, but not set, when you add it to the whipped cream and to ensure that your mixing bowl and whisk are extremely cold before you begin whipping the cream.

1 Put the stainless steel mixer bowl and whisk attachment in the freezer.

2 Put the water in a small bowl and sprinkle the gelatin over the surface. Let sit for at least 10 minutes.

3 In a small saucepan set over medium-low heat, bring ½ cup of the cream just to a simmer, 2 to 4 minutes. Pour the cream into the gelatin mixture and stir until the gelatin has dissolved. Refrigerate, stirring frequently, until cool but not set, about 8 minutes.

4 Remove the chilled bowl and whisk attachment from the freezer. In the electric mixer, beat the remaining 1½ cups heavy cream until it thickens just slightly, about 30 seconds. Add the sugar, vanilla bean paste, and salt and beat for 10 seconds. Very gradually add the gelatin mixture and beat until medium-firm peaks form, 1 to 2 minutes.

5 The frosting will keep in an airtight container in the refrigerator for up to 2 days.

VARIATIONS

» **Berry Whipped Cream Frosting:** Beat up to ⅓ cup (80 ml) seedless berry puree into the prepared frosting.

» **Chocolate Whipped Cream Frosting:** Sift 3 tablespoons (20 g) cocoa powder and add to the cream to be warmed in the saucepan, stirring to dissolve.

» **Lavender Whipped Cream Frosting:** Reduce the vanilla paste or extract to ½ teaspoon and add ¼ teaspoon culinary lavender extract (I like Star Kay White brand).

» **Lemon Whipped Cream Frosting:** Beat up to ⅓ cup (80 ml) lemon curd (see page 197 for instructions) into the prepared frosting.

» **Peppermint Whipped Cream Frosting:** Substitute the vanilla with 1½ teaspoons pure peppermint extract.

GLOSSY FUDGE FROSTING

MAKES ABOUT 4 CUPS

Dark, glossy, and super-chocolaty, this one is for serious chocolate lovers. I find the key to making this frosting is using the best quality cocoa powder you can find, as it really is the star of the show. The generous amount of cocoa powder gives this frosting a decadent dark chocolate hue and intense flavor, and a little hit of corn syrup adds a glossy finish.

1 cup (225 g) unsalted butter, room temperature

4 cups (500 g) confectioners' sugar

1 cup (120 g) best-quality Dutch-process dark cocoa powder (I like Cacao Barry Extra Brute)

⅓ cup (80 ml) milk

¼ cup (60 ml) water

1 tablespoon light corn syrup

2 teaspoons pure vanilla extract

¼ teaspoon pure almond extract

Pinch of salt

1 In the bowl of an electric mixer fitted with the paddle attachment, beat the butter on medium speed until very pale and creamy, 8 minutes.

2 Meanwhile, sift together the confectioners' sugar and cocoa powder. Reduce the mixer speed to low and gradually add the confectioners' sugar mixture, followed by the milk, water, corn syrup, vanilla, almond extract, and salt. Beat for 1 minute. Increase the speed to medium and beat until fluffy, about 3 minutes.

3 The frosting will keep in an airtight container in the refrigerator for up to 3 days. When ready to use, bring it to room temperature and beat on low speed to bring it back to spreadable consistency.

SHINY CHOCOLATE GLAZE

MAKES ABOUT 1 CUP

Super-shiny and chocolaty, this glaze is perfect for pouring over cakes for a dramatic effect. It also works well for dipping cookies, drizzling over frosted cupcakes, or spreading over almost any kind of square or bar that you want to "chocola-fy."

5 ounces (150 g) best-quality dark chocolate, chopped or callets/discs (I use Callebaut)

¾ cup (170 g) unsalted butter

1 tablespoon light corn syrup

Pinch of salt

In a medium heatproof bowl set over barely simmering water, melt the chocolate, butter, corn syrup, and salt until smooth, stirring occasionally. Remove the bowl from the heat and let cool slightly. The glaze will keep in an airtight container in the refrigerator for up to 1 week. When ready to use, warm the glaze in the microwave or over a pan of simmering water.

VARIATIONS

- **Mocha Glaze:** Add ½ teaspoon instant espresso powder.
- **Root Beer Glaze:** Stir in ¾ teaspoon root beer flavor oil or 2 teaspoons root beer extract.

CHOCOLATE GANACHE

MAKES ABOUT 3 CUPS

Your ganache will only ever be as good as the chocolate you put in it. You can use any kind of chocolate, but the darker it is, the more intense the ganache. I like to use a semisweet chocolate with 53% cocoa solids, as I find any darker is a bit too intense. It works beautifully as a filling or frosting, where you can show off its super-shiny and luscious finish.

10 ounces (300 g) best-quality dark chocolate, chopped or callets/discs (I use Callebaut)

1½ cups (360 ml) heavy cream

1 tablespoon glucose or light corn syrup

Pinch of salt

2 tablespoons unsalted butter, room temperature

1 tablespoon pure vanilla extract (or other desired extract)

1 Put the chocolate in a medium heatproof bowl and set aside.

2 In a medium saucepan set over medium heat, bring the heavy cream, glucose, and salt to a boil. Quickly pour the mixture over the chocolate. Let sit for about 1 minute, and then, using an immersion blender or a whisk, blend until smooth and shiny. Add the butter and vanilla and blend until super-smooth, 1 more minute. Let the ganache come to room temperature before chilling. Refrigerate the ganache until it reaches a thick-but-spreadable consistency, about 30 minutes. If it gets too thick, warm it slightly over a pot of barely simmering water until it reaches the desired consistency.

3 The ganache will keep covered in the refrigerator for up to 1 week.

VARIATIONS

- **Chocolate Orange Ganache:** Substitute the vanilla with orange liqueur (such as Grand Marnier).

- **Hazelnut Ganache:** Substitute the vanilla with hazelnut liqueur (such as Frangelico).

- **Milk Chocolate Ganache:** Reduce the heavy cream to 1 cup (240 ml) and substitute the dark chocolate with best-quality milk chocolate.

- **Mocha Ganache:** Stir 2 teaspoons instant espresso powder into the cream before heating.

- **Raspberry Ganache:** Substitute the vanilla with raspberry liqueur (such as Chambord).

- **Root Beer Ganache:** Replace the vanilla with ½ teaspoon root beer flavor oil or 1 tablespoon root beer extract.

- **Rum Ganache:** Substitute the vanilla with your favorite dark rum.

- **White Chocolate Ganache:** Reduce the heavy cream to 1 cup (240 ml) and substitute the dark chocolate with best-quality white chocolate. Let thicken until cool and then refrigerate until spreadable.

- **Whipped Ganache:** Once at room temperature, beat the ganache with an electric mixer using the whisk attachment until just thick and fluffy, about 20 seconds (don't over-beat or the ganache will become grainy).

SALTED CARAMEL

MAKES 1 CUP

Aside from being off-the-charts addictive and decadent, homemade caramel is extremely versatile. It can be added to buttercream, used to fill cupcakes, poured over ice cream, and so much more. This caramel recipe can be used to create a more fluid caramel sauce, or heated to a higher temperature to create a thicker, gooey caramel, ideal for spreading. If you've not yet made homemade caramel, it can seem a little intimidating, but it's a lot easier than it seems.

1 cup (200 g) granulated sugar

¼ cup (60 ml) water

½ teaspoon fresh lemon juice

¾ cup (180 ml) heavy cream

1 tablespoon unsalted butter

2 teaspoons vanilla bean paste or pure vanilla extract

¼ teaspoon flaked sea salt (I use fleur de sel)

TOOLS

Pastry brush

Candy thermometer

1 Put a heatproof bowl beside the stovetop. In a medium saucepan set over medium-low heat, combine the sugar, water, and lemon juice and stir to dissolve the sugar. Brush the down the sides of the saucepan with a dampened pastry brush and clip on a candy thermometer. Stop stirring. Increase the heat to medium-high and cook undisturbed until the mixture reaches a golden amber color, about 8 minutes. Promptly remove the saucepan from the heat and carefully stir in the cream and butter (be very careful, as it will bubble up and steam like crazy).

2 Return the saucepan to medium-high heat. To create a fluid caramel sauce that can be used to pour over ice cream or eaten by the spoonful (once cooled, that is), let the mixture bubble undisturbed until it reaches 240°F (116°C), about 2 minutes. Promptly remove the pan from the heat and pour the caramel into the heatproof bowl. Stir in the vanilla and sea salt, and let cool completely.

3 To create a thick, spreadable caramel, cook the caramel, undisturbed, until it reaches 248°F (120°C), also known as the firm ball stage, about 2 more minutes. Promptly remove the pan from the heat and pour the caramel into the heatproof bowl. Stir in the vanilla and sea salt, and let cool completely.

4 The caramel will keep sealed in a glass jar in the refrigerator for up to 1 week.

NOTES: The caramel will harden slightly in the refrigerator. Soften it for spreading by microwaving it in a heatproof bowl in 20-second intervals until it reaches the desired consistency. ◄ If you prefer a classic caramel, replace the sea salt with ½ teaspoon regular salt.

ROYAL ICING

MAKES ABOUT
2 CUPS

This pristine, snow-white icing is used not only for decorating fancy cookies but also for piping swags and borders on buttercream or fondant cakes (like the Neapolita Cake, page 90), as well as for making Homemade Sprinkles (page 16) and so much more. It also makes for a gorgeous cupcake icing, as it dries like porcelain and melts in your mouth. I use almond extract because it makes the icing taste like wedding cake, but you can use any extract you wish. If you are using the icing for decorating cookies or piping onto cakes (see page 133 for instructions), you will want to double the recipe.

4 cups (500 g) confectioners' sugar

¼ cup (40 g) meringue powder (see Note, page 196)

⅓ cup (80 ml) water, plus more for thinning

1 teaspoon fresh lemon juice, plus more for bowl

½ teaspoon pure almond extract (or extract of your choice)

AmeriColor gel paste food color (optional)

1   Wipe the stainless steel bowl and the paddle attachment of an electric mixer with a paper towel dampened with a little lemon juice to eliminate any trace of grease. Put the confectioners' sugar, meringue powder, ⅓ cup water, 1 teaspoon lemon juice, and extract in the bowl and beat on low speed until the ingredients have been incorporated. If the mixture is too dry, add a tablespoon or more water and continue to beat until very thick, 15 minutes. At this stage, the icing will be at a stiff-peak consistency, ideal for piping thick borders or other decorations.

2   For soft-peak icing, ideal for piping dots, lines, and other patterns: add a few drops of water and stir until the icing is glossy and looks like thick whipped cream.

3   For the perfect cookie-decorating or pourable cupcake icing consistency: add very small increments of water (a few drops at a time) until it reaches a "10-second" consistency. This means that a knife dragged through the middle of the icing will leave a line that flows back together and becomes invisible in 10 seconds.

RECIPE CONTINUES

stiff-peak

soft-peak

10-second

NOTES: You've likely seen some royal icing recipes that call for real egg whites, as opposed to meringue powder. While egg whites make for a satiny icing, I've noticed that the icing holds moisture, even once it should be completely "dry." This can be a problem when you're decorating cookies with intense colors that have the potential to bleed into one another. I also prefer meringue powder because it eliminates the concern in serving uncooked egg whites.

▨ If you find that your meringue powder has created a slightly off-white tinge to your otherwise angel-white icing, you can beat in a tablespoon of AmeriColor Bright White gel paste food color.

▨ Some meringue powder is gritty, and some brands are much more powder-like in consistency. I like Ateco brand meringue powder.

This consistency is ideal for outlining and filling the surface of cutout cookies.

4 Keep the icing tightly covered with plastic wrap or a damp cloth at all times because it dries out quickly.

5 The icing will keep covered with plastic wrap in the refrigerator for up to 3 days. When you're ready to use it again, give it a few stirs with a rubber spatula.

VARIATIONS

▨ **Black Velvet Royal Icing:** Omit the lemon juice and the extract. Add 1½ teaspoons Red Velvet Bakery Emulsion (see Note, page 157) and 1 teaspoon AmeriColor Super Black gel paste food color.

▨ **Chocolate Royal Icing:** Replace ⅓ cup (45 g) of the confectioners' sugar with ⅓ cup (40 g) cocoa powder.

▨ **Coffee Royal Icing:** Add ½ teaspoon instant espresso powder.

▨ **Cotton Candy Royal Icing:** Omit the lemon juice and the extract. Add ¼ teaspoon cotton candy flavor oil.

▨ **Red Velvet Royal Icing:** Omit the lemon juice and extract. Add 1½ teaspoons Red Velvet Bakery Emulsion (see Note, page 157). Add some AmeriColor Super Red gel paste food color to boost the shade of red, if desired.

▨ **Vanilla Bean Royal Icing:** Replace the almond extract with the seeds of ½ vanilla bean or 1 teaspoon vanilla bean paste.

ZINGY CITRUS CURD

MAKES ABOUT
2¼ CUPS

I could literally eat an entire batch of citrus curd with a spoon and a smile on my face. With its super-tart-and-sweet taste and silky smooth texture, it is pure lemon bliss. You can use it to fill cakes and cupcakes; spoon it onto pancakes, waffles, or crêpes; add it to vanilla buttercream or even cheesecake for an instant hit of zing; and so much more.

**6 lemons or oranges, or
9 Meyer lemons or limes**

**4 large eggs plus 6 large
yolks**

**1 cup (200 g) granulated
sugar**

**¾ cup (170 g) unsalted butter,
cut into cubes**

1 Wash the citrus really well, and using a zester, grate the zest from 1 lemon (be careful not to remove the bitter white pith); set the zest aside. Juice all of the lemons until you have ⅔ cup (170 ml) of juice. Strain the juice into a medium metal bowl and add the eggs, egg yolks, and sugar.

2 Set the bowl over a saucepan of simmering water. Whisk the mixture until smooth. Add the butter. Using a heatproof rubber spatula or a wooden spoon, stir the mixture gently until all of the butter has melted and the curd has thickened, 15 to 20 minutes. The curd should coat the back of your spatula. Strain the curd through a fine-mesh sieve into a bowl. Stir in the zest. Cover with plastic wrap pressed against the surface of the curd (to prevent a skin from forming) and refrigerate for at least 3 hours or overnight.

3. The curd will keep in an airtight container in the refrigerator for up to 1 week, or in the freezer for up to 6 months.

CANDY CLAY

MAKES 17 OUNCES (500 G)

Okay, whoa, this stuff is fun! Candy clay is essentially a candy coating (aka candy melts or moulding wafers) version of modeling chocolate. This candy-sweet, pliable dough behaves much like Play-Doh and can be used for everything from decorating cookies to making structured cake-decorating patterns. It is similar to fondant in that they both are sweet, sugary forms of dough, that can be molded, rolled, cut, and more; but unlike fondant, candy clay has very minimal stretch and does not fade or dry out when exposed to air.

When it comes to the brand of candy coating, I find some of the Merckens shades are much more vibrant than Wilton or Make 'n Mold; however, they all do a fine job as the base for the candy clay. For a paler shade, or custom colors, try experimenting with a mixture of colored melts with some white, or by combining any of the other colors.

---

14 ounces (400 g) candy coating in desired color

⅓ cup (110 g) light corn syrup (such as Karo)

2 tablespoons AmeriColor gel paste food color in Bright White (only if making white clay)

1 In a microwave-safe bowl, microwave the candy coating in 25-second intervals, stirring after each interval. Repeat until melted and smooth.

2 If making white clay, combine the corn syrup and Bright White gel paste, and microwave for 10 seconds; otherwise heat only the corn syrup. Add the corn syrup (or corn syrup mixture, if making white clay) to the candy coating and stir until blended and thick, about 30 strokes. Turn the clay out onto wax paper or plastic wrap and flatten it until it is about ½ inch thick. Let dry out for about 1 hour.

3 Knead the clay until it is smooth and pliable, about 1 minute. Put it in a well-sealed plastic zip-top bag. Let the clay sit overnight at room temperature before using.

4 The clay will keep sealed in a plastic zip-top bag indefinitely. To soften hardened clay, microwave for 7 to 10 seconds and knead until soft and shiny.

cakelets
IN THE KITCHEN

Needless to say, where there is smooth, shiny, rainbow-colored clay that smells of pure candy and chocolate, there are kids ready and eager to participate. Let them roll out their own candy clay and cut shapes for cupcakes, cookies, or even just for fun. This will keep them happily busy for hours while you work on your candy clay masterpiece.

VARIATIONS

- **Hot Pink Candy Clay:** Use Merckens brand pink (it is very bright).

- **Pastel Blue Candy Clay:** Use 9 ounces (260 g) white candy coating with 5 ounces (140 g) Merckens brand bright blue.

- **Pastel Lavender Candy Clay:** Use 9 ounces (260 g) white candy coating with 5 ounces (140 g) Merckens brand bright purple.

- **Pastel Pink Candy Clay:** Use 9 ounces (260 g) white candy coating with 5 ounces (140 g) Merckens brand pink.

- **Retro Orange Candy Clay:** Use 14 ounces (400 g) orange candy coating plus about 3 yellow plus 1 brown candy coating.

- **Shimmer Candy Clay:** Add luster dust for a shimmery effect.

- **Sprinkle Candy Clay:** Add a handful of rainbow jimmies or nonpareils to your set clay for a rainbow version.

- **Glitter Candy Clay:** Knead disco dust into prepared clay.

SIMPLE SYRUP

MAKES ABOUT
¾ CUP

While this super and, well, simple syrup is often found in the hands of mixologists behind cocktail bars, it is an extremely versatile addition to a baker's bag of tricks. With a sweet base of equal parts sugar and water, it lends itself to essentially any flavor you can dream up, which you can customize using extract, liqueur, spices, and more. A quick brush onto cake layers or cupcakes not only infuses the cake with flavor but also adds a sometimes much-needed hit of moisture (depending on the cake).

½ cup (100 g) granulated sugar

½ cup (120 ml) water

1 teaspoon flavor oil, or
2 teaspoons extract,
or 1 to 2 tablespoons liqueur
(optional)

1 In a small saucepan set over medium heat, bring the sugar and water to a boil. Cook until the syrup begins to thicken slightly, 2 minutes.

2 Remove the pan from the heat and stir in the flavor oil, if using. Let cool completely.

3 The syrup will keep covered in the refrigerator for up to 2 weeks.

INSTANT EDIBLE VARNISH

MAKES
1 CUP

For a quick and easy high-gloss lacquer for fondant, gum paste, royal icing, candy clay, and more, this instant varnish works wonders. Simply paint on one or two coats of the varnish using a food-safe paintbrush and let dry.

½ cup (160 g) light corn syrup

½ cup (120 ml) vodka

In a small container with a lid, combine the corn syrup and vodka. The varnish will keep in an airtight container at room temperature for up to 1 month.

CONFECTIONERS' GLAZE

MAKES ABOUT 1 CUP

It's rather amazing that two simple ingredients can simply be whisked together to create such a magical and versatile glaze. Whip it up when you want to add a sweet touch to cakes, cookies, or bars—it will firm up quickly and will be shiny and dry to the touch. Use the Confectioners' Coating variation when you want to create more of a shiny shell finish.

2½ cups (315 g) confectioners' sugar, sifted

6 tablespoons (90 ml) milk

In a medium bowl, whisk together the confectioners' sugar and milk until smooth. Keep covered until ready to use.

VARIATIONS

- **Flavored Glaze:** Add your favorite extract to taste, adding more confectioners' sugar if necessary to thicken.

- **Confectioners' Coating:** Whisk in 1 ounce (30 g) melted candy coating (aka moulding wafers) to create a shiny, dry coating for your cookies or bars. Choose a colored candy melt to tint your coating, if desired.

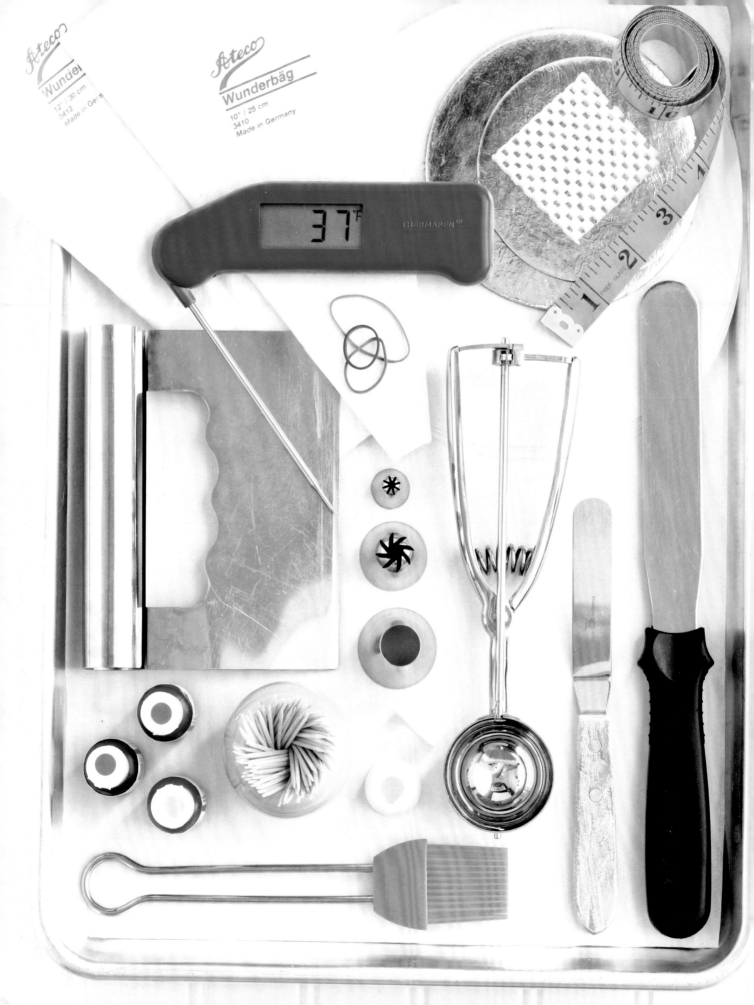

SOURCES

COLOR PALETTE INSPIRATION

Design Seeds (designseeds.com)
Perfect Palette (perfectpalette.com)

COOKIE CUTTERS

Copper Gifts (coppergifts.com)
Etsy (etsy.com)

FLAVOR OILS, BAKERY EMULSIONS, AND MORE

LorAnn Oils (lorannoils.com)

HANDMADE SUGAR FLOWERS

Flour Confections (flourconfections.ca)
Global Sugar Art (globalsugarart.com)

SPECIALTY BAKING AND CAKE-DECORATING SUPPLIES

Flour Confections (flourconfections.com)
Fancy Flours (fancyflours.com)
Global Sugar Art (globalsugarart.com)

PREMIUM INGREDIENTS

Amazon (amazon.com)
Golda's Kitchen (goldaskitchen.com)
Vanilla Food Company (vanillafoodcompany.ca)

SILICONE MOLDS

First Impression Molds (firstimpressionmolds.com)
Etsy (etsy.com)

SPRINKLES, SPARKLES, AND SUCH

Bulk Barn (across Canada)
Amazon (amazon.com)
Flour Confections (flourconfections.com)
Fancy Flours (fancyflours.com)
Golda's Kitchen (goldaskitchen.com)

STYLISH CAKE TOPPERS

Sweet and Saucy (sweetandsaucysupply.com)
Etsy (etsy.com)

VINTAGE AND KITSCHY BAKING AND PARTY SUPPLIES

Etsy (etsy.com)
Hey YoYo (heyyoyo.com)

ACKNOWLEDGMENTS

Heartfelt hugs and high fives to everyone who made this book possible, and who took part in making it the best it could be. I'd like to send sincere and sprinkle-covered thank-yous to these supportive folks:

The Sweetapolita website **readers**—you are the most devoted and passionate bakers in this sugar-filled universe. You have convinced me that baking is indeed a way of life, and you have given me the chance to call sprinkle-tossing my job. It is all of you who make this entire adventure possible. Let us bake!

Judy Linden, literary agent extraordinaire. You make me feel like a rock star. Not only did you believe in me from the beginning, you gave me such "tough love" advice along the way. Going way above and beyond, you answered all of my questions with such care (3 a.m. panicked author emails, anyone?). I am proud to call you my agent, but also my friend. Under your wing, I went from a girl with a dream to a published author. This book would not be this book without you and your wisdom, and I am forever grateful.

The entire team at **Clarkson Potter/Penguin Random House, Inc.**, with a special chocolate-covered thank-you to **Ashley Phillips** for being such an incredibly patient and talented editor. Your enthusiasm and invaluable feedback convinced me that I am doing what I am meant to do—I have learned so much from you (and I will likely resist the urge to type the words "nostalgic" and "really" for the rest of eternity!). And to the entire team at **Penguin Random House Canada**, with a super-sweet thank-you to **Robert McCullough**—you are such a warm and encouraging force, and I am honored to be a part of your ensemble of authors.

The best in-laws a girl could wish for, **Vic and Kathy Alyea** and **Frank and Mary Lou Kinsella**, thank you for taking such loving care of Reese and Neve, particularly over the past year and a half while I created this book. Not only did you give me the quiet time to bake and write, but you simultaneously created treasured "Grammy & Grandpa" and "Nanny & Papa" memories for the girls. Without you, this book (or Reese and Neve for that matter) would simply not exist, so thank you from the bottom of my heart. You mean the world to us.

My **Mom** for always nurturing my sensitive side, my creativity, and my love for sugary supermarket birthday cakes. Because of you, I bake from the heart.

My **Dad** for teaching me that if you're going to do something, it's best to do it right—and with flair. Thinking back to my days at home, watching you thoughtfully wrap a gift, set a table, or plate a dinner, reminds me that the sprinkle doesn't fall far from the cake.

To my husband, **Grant**, for enduring more cake-talk than any fitness enthusiast should ever have to, and for convincing me I look beautiful with no makeup, a batter-covered apron, and pink icing in my hair. When you baked me that fateful pink cherry cake more than eleven years ago, I knew I'd call you my husband. You have worked unthinkably hard to support our family while I pursue my dreams, and your generosity and support will never, ever be forgotten.

The Sheppards—Mary and Ted—for being a unique blend of friends, family, and flat-out awesome folk. Mar, not only do you listen to me whine and cheer me on with vigor, you make one heck of a hand model. Ted, you solved all of my techy and photography 911s with such patience. And sweet little **Teddy**, thank you for being the world's best baby while I photographed your mommy for an entire day—what must have seemed like an eternity in your world. You are a joy.

To my recipe testers, **Kristen and Vanessa Valencia**, for such thorough and helpful work, and for eating copious amounts of cake. You are the only girls I know who can whip up 6-layer cakes with such ease and mastery on the first go.

Finally, to my beloved cakelets, **Reese and Neve,** for being the shiniest stars in my universe and for being extraordinarily patient and understanding while Mommy wrote this book. Because of you, I get to see through the sparkly eyes of little girls and live with infinite happiness. I love you both more than sprinkle-covered cake.

TEMPLATES

Enlarge templates by 120%

Panda mask

Cat mask

Fox mask

INDEX